David,

Thanks for your support of the

Tax - Exempt Client Group.

Dave

SUPRA-CONSCIOUS LEADERSHIP

New Thinking For A New World

SUPRA-CONSCIOUS LEADERSHIP

New Thinking For A New World

JAMES N. FARR, PH.D.

R̄TP
RESEARCH TRIANGLE PUBLISHING

Published by
Research Triangle Publishing, Inc.
PO Box 1130
Fuquay-Varina, NC 27526

ISBN 1-884570-81-x

Editorial coordination: John Patrick Grace
Grace Associates, Ltd., at Publishers Place
945 Fourth Avenue, Suite 200A
Huntington, West Virginia 25701
Phone 304-697-3236

Jacket Design by Kathy Holbrook

Library of Congress Catalog Card Number: 97-76538

⊗ The paper used in this publication meets the minimum requirements of the
American National Standard for Information Sciences—Permanence of Paper
for Printed Library Materials, ANSI Z39,48-1984.

Printed in the United States of America
10 9 8 7 6 5 4 3 2 1

ACKNOWLEDGEMENTS

Over forty years of consulting as a Management Psychologist, from a teaching stint at New York University to directing the first stages of the Center for Creative Leadership to building Farr Associates, Inc., I have accumulated many intellectual debts to both colleagues and clients. Among those who have been especially instrumental in refining the concepts expressed in this book I would like to credit Rene Johnson, Leon Festinger, Stanley Schachter, and John Grinnell, and Dennis Quaintance for his constant encouragement to "get it written."

Patrick Grace, a versatile writer and editor, worked with me for the last four years of developing this text, with welcome insights from Marc Jaffe for improving the book's tone, and Bill Allen added incisive editing and restructuring suggestions. Bonnie Tilson tightened the text with her astute line editing, and Kate Duncan backed me up with proofing. Trent True contributed significantly as a researcher of quotes, as did Dianne Wardlaw as the graphic artist who executed the construct figures. My daughter Sandra Heaton functioned as my faithful executive secretary for the project. To all of these fine people, I extend both a hearty "thank you" and an absolution from blame for any undersights or oversights in this text, for which the author alone accepts full responsibility.

—JNF

CONTENTS

FOREWORD

A very wise man, Will Rogers, once said that it's not the things we *don't know* that get us into trouble, "It's the things we know that *ain't so.*" In his long-awaited book on leadership, Jim Farr challenges us to recognize the biases and misconceptions that we established as children, to examine the conventional wisdom of our day, and to be aware of our own ego-driven barriers to new ideas and new ways of working with today's more educated and sophisticated workforce. Jim also gives us a set of guideposts for establishing professional standards for leaders—much like the standards that govern doctors and lawyers.

I've known Jim Farr since my company, First Union Corporation, looked over the horizon in about 1978 and saw a world of significant change and industry consolidation coming. By the mid 1980s, First Union was at a pivotal place in its history: Not only was the landscape changing rapidly through bank consolidation, but the competitive field, the regulatory environment, and even our customers were changing.

As a $7 billion bank in only one state, North Carolina, we were too small to compete with the encroaching competition from Wall Street. We were also too small to offer the variety of innovative products that our customers were demanding to help them provide for longer retirements and other life needs. We had a choice: 1) Sell the company—but in those days, there weren't many buyers interested in a $7 billion North Carolina bank; 2) Wait to be bought—but that seemed passive and defeatist, and not what we were about as a company; or 3) Pursue an active strategy of growth by acquisition ourselves. And that's what we did.

In the midst of our rapid expansion, however, I sensed something wasn't quite right. Somehow employees weren't always as enthusiastic as I was about the course we were pursuing; somehow they didn't seem as scared as I was of the consequences if First Union failed to achieve its goals. I started asking a blunt question of some of the best and brightest minds at all levels of our company: What was wrong? They answered that we had grown rapidly and knitted together a variety of conflicting cultures. Sometimes we did things in a very high-handed way, and a lot of individuals were getting lost in the process. Morale was low. Adding to my fears, I knew that we were only at the beginning of a long process of necessary change. In terms of a marathon, we were only at the two-mile marker. It wasn't a matter of getting more productivity out of our employees—we were already one of the most productive banks I knew. But I looked to the future, and I feared that our good, hard-working people were unprepared to operate in a world where the old way of waiting until customers walked in the door was no longer valid. We had to change our "order-taking" mindset and stop operating on auto-pilot. From top to bottom, we needed a common mindset that was eager to actively sell and serve our customers—something virtually unheard of then in a bank.

In our rush for efficiency in a period of rapid growth, we had to be most mindful to keep our main focus where it needed to be: on our customers' best interests. And we had to do that while continuing to evolve into something new that was no longer just a "bank," because the competition was getting more varied and innovative every day. In other words, what had worked for us so far, what had brought us to our successful position, nevertheless would not work in the future. At the same time, we had to earn the trust of our workforce that we were not oblivious, as leaders, to the pain caused by having to change so rapidly.

Most of all, we had to build a culture that welcomed—even embraced—change as the only way to endure as a lasting, flexible, adaptable enterprise.

At the same time, I realized that we had to find a way to keep the humanity in our company, no matter how large we might become. As leaders, we had to commit ourselves to paying as much attention to the personal growth of our colleagues as we did to growing our company. For me, work has to be about more than a paycheck. As Studs Terkel once wrote memorably, "Work is about daily meaning as well as daily bread." This is the right attitude for the soul of our corporation, and it is also, frankly, enlightened self interest for a corporate leader—because developing and nurturing the individual is the key to long-term organizational success. So, in order to earn the trust we needed to lead our company into the future, we had to help each individual grow and find challenging work, to give each employee a sense that he or she was contributing daily to something of enduring value. We had first to understand, anticipate and satisfy the needs of a growing workforce if we were going to understand, anticipate and satisfy the needs of our customers. But how could we communicate, from top to bottom, the values we had as a company, and let people know that these values were not lip service, but real, daily functioning ways we approached our business?

First Union began sending leaders to Farr Associates. The results were good, and so we sent more and more. Over the past two decades, several thousand First Union employees have gone through Farr's leadership development programs. We also have used Jim Farr as an internal consultant for upper-level executives. In fact, my own leadership weekend at Farr Associates still ranks as the most meaningful—and most emotional—leadership experience of my entire career. It really helped me to begin understanding how my emotions and my intellect interact.

Not the least of benefits to First Union has been that Jim Farr has helped us build a common language for discussion, for breaking down turf protection and for combating the silos of self-centered management that spring up between divisions. It's often true that good managers burn out or lose their effectiveness after twenty or so years in management. They are still doing the same things they always did—but those things are no longer effective in interacting with a less homogeneous work force that hasn't had the same life experiences as the veteran managers had. With Farr's ever-present challenge to us to make sure our management and our mindsets evolve, our managers have been able to be effective over the long term. I truly believe that Farr is the key reason that other organizations are attracted to merging with us: Other people say First Union has "more heart" than most other organizations have. There's no question that Farr has benefitted First Union's bottom line and strategic prospects.

In this important book, Jim Farr seeks to do for the world what he has done for hundreds of individuals and corporate leaders: Increase our understanding of what really counts, and focus our attention on working for the greater good, not just for our own self interest. Jim has given us the mile markers, in a series of tenets of leadership, for our journey toward a company, a community, a country and a world that realizes that while leaders are necessary as an integrating and directing force, these same leaders are obliged to hold followers' lives and future in sacred trust. *"Our" leadership, as Jim reinforces throughout this book, has been created by the needs of the people and exists as a service to the people we lead.*

All of us would do well to take that lesson to heart...in fact, to infuse it into our nervous systems, so that the decisions we circulate as leaders are made with the full knowledge of the impact these decisions have on each individual we lead. We are privileged to lead, but with that privilege comes responsibility to those who trust us to make decisions not for our own self interest, but with a sense of concern and compassion for all whom our decisions affect. We are obliged to be aware of the ripple effects on our employees, on their families, on our communities and on our world for the leadership paths we take and the decisions we make. In Jim Farr's vision, the phrase "If you can change your mind, you can change the world" is more than a platitude. It is a clarion call for enlightened leadership so that we may all survive in a world that is more hospitable to all of humanity and all of the planet. I hope that more decision makers will listen to this remarkable leader as he talks to us about true leadership.

Edward E. Crutchfield
Chairman and CEO
First Union Corporation
Charlotte, North Carolina
January 23, 1998

Human life is the rarest, most complex, and most precious of all the prizes in the universe. It is this prize that is now in the process of being diminished and rejected— by humans themselves. Humans are tampering with the vital fractions that made their existence possible. It becomes necessary, therefore, to develop a survival perspective. We must think in ways we have never thought before—about our uniqueness, about our place in the universe, about the preciousness of life, about value, about our relationship to other human beings, about the new institutions or mechanisms that are required to deal with random and pulverizing power, and about the rights of the next generation.

—Norman Cousins
Human Options, 1981

SUPRA-CONSCIOUS LEADERSHIP

NEW THINKING FOR A NEW WORLD

Chapter One

OF THINGS THAT NEVER WERE

You see things and you say, "Why?"
I dream things that never were and I say, "Why not?"
                                    —George Bernard Shaw

We ARE INUNDATED TODAY with calls for "New Leadership." These calls come from everywhere imaginable—politicians, business executives, academics, merchants, police officials, and just plain citizens. The average American has been aware for some time that we need more and better leadership in our society. We spend time hiding from crime. We worry about the rationality of a government that often seems to expend more energy downgrading the character of political opponents than it does on issues. We listen to endless squabbles over welfare and health benefits. We watch the illegal drug business boom despite our constant efforts to stop it. We wonder what is wrong with our school system that turns out students poorly equipped to compete with those of other developed nations. We are horrified by repeated episodes of genocide in states around the world. We may not know exactly what good leadership is, but we look at the world and are well aware that there isn't enough of it.

Society is pregnant with an imperative for change: change in perceptions, attitudes, and resulting actions. The trouble is, with the state the world is in, the birth of change is not likely to occur without a Caesarean section. From various quarters voices suggest paths toward society-saving leadership. The calls for such leadership are on target: we do indeed need change. More directly, we need leaders who can bring about change. Most of all, *we need leaders to lead the leaders; to lead the process of changing leadership* and create a new and more vibrant society.

How do we go about changing the leaders who can then change leadership to usher in the critical improvements we need for our increasingly complex and challenging society? This book responds to that question. It explores a number of important human and societal problems, and searches for solutions from an uncommon perspective.

Leaders' current ways of operating derive from traditional understandings of what they are supposed to do and how they should exercise their authority. Therefore, it stands to reason that for change to occur, old programs, old mindsets, (also known as mental models) must be jettisoned and new programs that define how the world works will have to be integrated into leaders' mental filing systems. Unfortunately, in view of the way egos work, there undoubtedly will be a great deal of resistance to any call for such jettisoning of highly valued ideas. It's not that we have failed to make progress toward learning new mindsets that would enable us to confront and deal with our complex new social quandaries; rather the reality is that too few people have brought themselves to the point of undertaking such mindset changes. The rate at which such changes take place is *much too slow!* This results in what I call "leadership-lag," a phenomenon that could prove disastrous in our society if something isn't done soon to heighten leaders' awareness and promote *faster* change and *more* change.

Through the years I have had thousands of leaders, from hundreds of companies and public-sector units, go through Leadership Development and Self-Awareness Workshops at Farr Associates in Greensboro, North Carolina. Nine out of ten of those leaders arrived believing, if they thought about it at all, that leadership was something that could be learned like mathematics or computer science. They did not understand that becoming a genuine leader would require a dramatic and often threatening plunge into the vortex of the mind—their own minds in particular and the human mind in general. But it does require such an experience. It is heartening to note that all but the most stubbornly resistant participants in our workshops finally came to see and accept this.

By the happenstance of my childhood I came to experience such a plunge into the vortex of my mind early in life. I grew up in a country backwoods area of western Washington. My neighbors had little education. They were blue-collar workers or subsistence farmers. My family was on relief during the depression; I attended a four-room elementary school and stayed close to home. I seldom even visited a town. When I was fourteen, we moved into a small town where I took my place in the low-income blue-collar community. I did not think of this situation as unusual, of course, for I was in the only social climate I had ever known. I went to high school and was more or less ignored by my so-called peers because I didn't have the vaguest idea of how to fit in.

When I was seventeen, a wealthy uncle I had never seen came from Minnesota to ask whether I wanted to go to college. I asked him, "What's *that?*" After he explained it to me, I decided that I wanted to go because I had a vague notion that college was a path to a better way of living; so I said "yes." Two days later my uncle sent me a ticket, and I put myself on a train bound for Minneapolis. There I took up residence in the affluent country club section of the city. I began the process of getting into classes at the University of Minnesota.

I quickly found my new circumstances strange and confusing. I discovered the people around me were experiencing a very different world from the world as I knew it. The way my mind saw things was not the way things seemed to be for these people, not at all. Their interpretations of what was good and bad, right and wrong, dull and interesting were far from my interpretations that were shaped by my backwoods, blue-collar, impoverished childhood conditioning. Their rules for manners, relationships, and goals, and their hierarchy of what was important in life astonished me. Nevertheless, I began to adjust my mindsets to fit in with *their* reality. After all, I lived among those people; I had little alternative.

As I paid attention to their ways of interpreting the world, it became startlingly clear to me that my mindsets—my beliefs, values, and attitudes about reality—produced experiences that were very different from the experience of that same reality my classmates, teachers, and staff at the university were creating. As uneducated as I was, I became vividly aware that a good part of the facts and truths in my mind were all made up; they were not dictated by the nature of the world. I concluded that we human beings make up our view of reality in accord with the circumstances of our lives.

This vivid discovery resonated through my consciousness as I moved into my freshman year of studies. I had initially decided to major in journalism, but I accidentally enrolled in a beginning course in psychology. I was soon fascinated with the opportunity to learn more about the human mind and how it creates reality. I changed my major to psychology. My years of study confirmed for me the view I still hold: human beings are *not* their minds; they create their minds to conform to the logic that their life experience has instilled. In turn, their minds then shape the reality of what they experience "out there."

Understanding such processes of the mind is a critical element that is widely overlooked in leadership studies and practices. This oversight accounts for one of the common problems I run across in my leadership development work; leaders endeavor to get people to follow them by leading from their executive minds, generally based on privileged backgrounds and considerable formal education. Yet many of the people these executives or managers are trying to lead are individuals who have grown up in much the same environment as I had. And even when the leader and followers have grown up in similar environments, they often have widely varying needs and values that control their perception of reality. In other words, leaders and followers often live in very different psychological worlds. The confusion that results seldom is seen by leaders to be the product of the differences in mindsets.

In some ways a mind can be compared to a radio. The universe is full of music that comes to a person from outside sources, but that music is not available to be experienced unless the person has a radio. Music comes into the radio from the outside as radio waves. The radio transforms these impulses into a sound that can be heard by the human ear, so that one can delight in anything from Beethoven to Sting. Some from a primitive culture might look at a radio and think it produces the music, but in reality, that's not the case. The radio is merely *channeling* the music.

Like a radio, the mind is the instrument that brings the outside world into a consciousness. The mind receives external stimuli which range from auditory to visual to tactile. These stimuli prompt us to think or judge or react in a great many ways, *which are almost always congruent with the mindsets we create through our educational, social, and moral conditioning.* Our mind receives the stimuli, then processes them through our mindsets (programs or mental models). The result is the world as the mind perceives it—not necessarily as it may actually be. We have the same reality but different perceptions of that reality. What is more, each mind triggers reactions in accord with those differing perceptions. (This is clearly demonstrated by the situation of two people dealing with a third party who one sees as attractive or interesting while the other sees as unattractive or dull.)

The culture creates beliefs, and then the beliefs create the culture. This interaction helps create a stable society— and also makes it difficult to solve some of the culture's problems that afflict the minority. It also means that when the slow evolutionary, rate of social change gives way to a rapid, transformational rate of change, as has occurred in recent years, we have a problem. Because minds work to sustain their programs and to resist change, we end up with leaders applying old programs to new problems.

There may be fifty stations out there, but if your radio has only ten channels, you will only experience ten stations. And if our minds do not have channels or programs capable of receiving new aspects of our culture, then, as both leaders and followers, we will have difficulty receiving and dealing with what is new. For example, a white man with our culture's old prejudicial program perceives and reacts differently to a man who is white than he does to one who is black. He creates different experiences on the basis of his programmed beliefs, despite national efforts to instill a belief that all men are created equal. For another example, despite the fact that we have moved so far from the edge of survival that we can produce enough to enable everyone to live in comfort and safety, we still tend to run the world from win-lose mindsets.

Through its programs, as well as channeling inputs from the outer world, the mind also channels the inputs that come from one's higher self. The mind translates our being energy into our personhood. Fundamentally, the mind is the instrument through which the inner being expresses its aliveness. However, many of us tend to deny the link between the inner being and the conscious mind, with the result that we program ourselves more and more from ego, which is mind's propensity to assume that it (the mind) is all there is. We assume that our way of understanding the world is the only way to understand it. Training that would teach us all to keep that channel open would infuse our world with a great deal more of the inventiveness and compassion of the higher self.

The "social mind" of the society we live in is a conglomeration of billions of individual minds. These minds are greatly influenced by upbringing, cultural context, and education. Such life experiences are the primary influences that shape our programs and beliefs. However, as we grow older and accumulate programs, we are likely to add to them in another way. Based on the existing programs, we reason our way to new ones, but these new programs are merely expansions or additions to what already exists. Thus, if one has strong programming to the effect that one race of people is inferior to another, the only new programs that will be accepted will be those that conform to that position. The new program, therefore, is nothing but a once-removed reflection of past experience. No new life experience has been involved in shaping the new position other than the automated thinking that brought it into focus. It follows, therefore, that unless we get off automatic pilot, as we meet new problems and challenges, we will perceive, reflect, and choose courses of action based on the ways our minds were shaped in early life. It does not take a great stretch of imagination to see how many of the problems that beset our society arise because millions of individuals go through their days dealing with what they see, hear, and feel from a wide range of vastly differing programs.

The resulting social mind sometimes produces harmony, but too frequently there is clashing as we bring widely varying minds to bear on problems that require unified action in their solutions. For example, peace is not possible when one group of people tries to dominate another. An organization cannot succeed in achieving its objectives if the members do not agree on the objectives. The world seems to be full of righteous confusion; righteous because both parties in a conflict are *absolutely certain* their views are right and the other party's views are wrong.

Following the collapse of the Berlin Wall, West Germans were euphoric about reuniting their country. Soon, however, it became clear to West German officials and citizens that a thoroughly different culture, manifested by different mindsets, had taken root in East Germany while under Communist rule. East Germans were not nearly so inclined to make their own way through ingenuity, thrift, and hard work, as were the West Germans. Rather they had become used to living off the largesse of the state; they had grown accustomed to working only as hard as was necessary to avoid punishment or loss of privileges, and they had become quite docile in accepting the state's control over virtually every aspect of their lives. The East Germans were literally not ready for the responsibilities of democracy and enterprise. Their mindsets did not fit that kind of reality. Reacculturating East Germans to the free-enterprise West, it was soon evident, would involve intensive reeducation over a number of years.

We need to note the sort of special attention that Germany is now giving to the challenge of bringing East Germans back into the fold, into a consciousness of what it means to be free, responsible, and productive members of a free community. This example gives us a clue as to what must be done on a global scale, to promote mindset changes among both leaders and followers that will enable us to move more precisely and thoughtfully toward solving the problems of our evolving culture. The problem is magnified by virtue of the rapid pace of society's development both in size and in complexity. We court disaster and destruction of society's patterns and operations if we wait mindlessly upon a normal evolution of new mindsets. *Like Germany, we must give special attention to the goal of altering consciousness for ourselves and for our peers, and the mind changes we engineer should be determined and focused according to a well-thought-out plan for the objectives we wish to achieve in our society.*

Deliberate mind changing requires an increase in social self-consciousness. This will enable us to better see ourselves, not as isolated individual corporate divisions, cities, or even states, but as individuals who form part of families and other groups, departments that make up corporations, cities that form part of a region, and states that form part of the community of nations. In short, it will enable us to see ourselves as part of a unity, *part of a social organism.*

What keeps people from becoming more self-aware? It's the same thing that keeps the social organism from developing better social self-consciousness. What stops us is the habit of getting lost in our mindsets and programs—those mental models that fit earlier times, but do not fit new situations. These older programs consist of beliefs, values, attitudes, morals, and ethics that are no longer suited to resolving present-day problems. Our world has grown dramatically and our programs have not kept pace with this growth. We have experienced rapid growth in population, and we have breakdowns in our institutions such as our churches, our schools, and our courts. However, ego being what it is—trying to maintain itself as "right"—makes it difficult for even well-educated and progressive individuals, people we consider to be the thinkers and main movers of our society, to come to the realization that they need to change their minds. They are still drowsing under a cloud of illusions from the past, illusions that do not fit the present.

The first of these illusions is that the leadership style we now use, or see others use, is the kind that will provide what we need to cope with whatever tomorrow may bring. *It will not.* Another illusion is the belief that the present rate of improving and changing societal awareness is in step with the rapid social changes that are challenging us to find new ways of being and doing. From where I sit, it is clear that the current evolution of mindsets is definitely *not* in step with the mounting challenges we now face.

To appreciate the nature of true leadership, we have to get outside ourselves, outside our restricting cultural prejudices, outside our ego, and develop a more *dis*passionate and *com*passionate world-view. That so few people have been able to achieve this goal goes far toward explaining much of our current social malaise. Things are the way they are because almost everybody has been viewing the world from a limited, selfish perspective. For the world to change—for us to cut back on the threats of pollution, crime, stress and depression, unresolved budget deficits, and rank poverty—leaders have to *considerably* expand their awareness. We cannot solve many of our social problems without strong leadership.

This book will help you develop new mindsets that more appropriately fit current society and put you in closer touch with your inner self. Such a change inevitably makes one a better leader, more fully human and compassionate, and better equipped to contribute productively to building and supporting society. Bringing about such a change is a matter of seeing the world you now think you know from a different perspective.

Making this happen requires you to build many new mindsets. To get society on a track more suited to our transformed world requires that a great many people build those new mindsets. *One stumbling block is that most who must lead us into the new mindsets are themselves still stuck in the old mindsets!* What people "see" tends to fit their current mindsets, the mindsets they are comfortable with. What does not fit those mindsets—and makes you uncomfortable—you tend to reject because your ego resists new mindsets that contradict the ones that sustain your sense of comfort, rightness, and safety.

To change mindsets by design, thoughtfully and immediately rather than through the slow process of trial-and-error, requires *us to manage our egos, rather than be managed by them.* Ego is in charge when you automatically follow the programs already in place in your mind. In essence, that means you are operating as if you were your mind. However, you are *not* your mind; you are a powerful being expressed *through* your mind. The distinction is critical. The mind's function is to ensure the survival of the being. It does this by maintaining *right programs for survival.*

The percentage of leaders who are open to the concepts you'll soon encounter in this book is small, but it is growing. We need their openness if we are to ensure social health, and perhaps even our survival as a global village. Without leaders' willingness to learn to change, to adapt to new realities, the world as we know it is in danger of self-destructing, and neither this nor any other book, nor movement, nor religion will be able to prevent it. We must adapt our behaviors to the needs of the massive society we are creating, and we cannot adapt our behaviors until we change our minds.

My ideas have evolved out of forty years as a professional psychologist consulting with leaders in business, the military, and government—experience spanning most of the American states and some foreign countries. In the early years, my work centered on teaching leadership skills and techniques. Clients began to ask me to help executives and management teams gain more cooperation and production from their people, and improve the overall quality of the organization. I excitedly tackled these problems on the basis of the mindsets I incorporated from my background and brought my solutions to the situation. As I gained experience, however, I became increasingly concerned that the mindsets I was applying to the issues were no longer appropriate. This carried me back to my early days in Minnesota as I reexperienced a clash between my backwoods mindsets and those of my new Minnesota friends. I became more and more concerned that the mechanical performance improvements that I was helping bring about often resulted in negative effects on the lives and beings of the client organizations and their employees. I became troubled as I watched leaders move enthusiastically, based on their old mindsets, toward one goal or another, with no apparent awareness that their policies and actions were creating unhappy and undermotivated employees. One of the simplest examples I remember was in a foundry where management happily and proudly worked for a year to automate the production line. Until production on the new line fell below what it was for the old line, management leaders were totally unaware that what they were doing was frightening and angering the employees who worked the line.

So I added to my approach. I looked for ways to find new mindsets more appropriate to the problems I was facing. I began to teach that leadership always has three objectives: 1) effective organization, 2) the well-being of the employees who produce the work and the customers it serves, and 3) the good of the society that it affects. While some clients rejected this "humanistic" approach, a great many responded positively. Those who did were leaders who had simply not been aware of the negative effects of their goal-oriented leadership, and whose humanity would not allow them to keep on with those hurtful practices after they became aware of their effects.

With more experience, my perspective broadened more. It dawned on me that everything a leader does with his or her people has an impact on their lives. I saw that millions of executives and politicians who lead us in the work world and in government shape the experiences that shape our attitudes, expectations, morale, ethics, and habits. It is well known that people are shaped through their years in school. It is not so commonly recognized that significant shaping of mind and personality results from the effects of the leadership we receive everywhere, especially in our work lives. I began to observe that the leadership methods being used in the work force were destroying the very work ethic upon which the organization depended.

I was even more startled to see that the by-products of the leadership we have too long accepted included such things as destruction of the ozone layer, the pollution of our streams, lakes, and ocean, acid rain destruction of our forest, and paranoid relationships among nations.

Finally, even that observation fell short of reality: I soon realized that those ruinous effects are not merely by-products of leadership, they are often direct effects of policy set in place by leaders. Effects of which we have been unaware. *Effects for which our leaders have not held themselves accountable.* Far too many leaders have limited their accountability to the immediate effects of their work. They have failed to see that it is not possible to lead any body of people whether at the neighborhood, city, national or world level, without at the same time contributing, either positively or negatively, to the general context of society. Since their leadership is part of the leadership-element that acts as the glue that holds society together, that is a dangerously shortsighted perspective.

The growth in mass and complexity of society has transformed the nature of the social needs that require leadership. Things at our present stage of development are such that our survival as human beings, and the survival of the life-sustaining systems of the planet, depend upon operations directed by leaders.

This is a sobering realization if we stop to think about the horrific examples of mismanagement and myopic leadership of which our world has recently been a victim. We've had business leaders negotiating mergers or takeovers to serve the interests of a few hundred stockholders, themselves included, of course, while they simultaneously saddled a company with crippling debt, laid off thousands of workers, and even debilitated whole towns or regions. Insider trading deals and other scandals have run rampant on Wall Street and poisoned the business climate. Political leaders have abused their power to trample on their people, they have used citizens as pawns in power games, they have led assaults on neighboring states, and they have created vile programs of "ethnic cleansing."

Such ills proceed, I believe, from one basic problem: most leaders (like everybody else) tend to perceive the world automatically on the basis of the way their minds are set. They launch themselves into actions based on their perceptions of what is out there in "reality." Rarely do they stop to challenge the perceptions and thoughts that lead to their response. They do not evaluate their minds to determine whether the mindsets (or "programs") in place are good matches for situations, or whether other mindsets might engender better approaches. Put another way, these leaders are unaware of their minds as *programmed structures;* instead, they are focused on the *products* of their minds. They are aware of *what* they think rather than of *how* they think.

Leaders who take their minds and mindsets for granted do not examine their own implicit assumptions about human interactions before they go through the process of analyzing problems and creating the leadership concepts and approaches to deal with them. They merely view the world from their preprogrammed mind and launch a leadership program that is in harmony with their unchallenged mind. As they become leaders, they change their mindsets only in the sense that they go through learning processes and add programs to carry out actions. They ensure that the added programs support their "tried and true" mindsets. They make the automatic and implicit assumption that their mindsets are appropriate, and then go on to fool themselves into believing that if they merely learn the *content and form* of leadership actions, they will be good leaders. They are wrong.

One consequence of leaders being unaware of their mindsets is that most of them then lead on the basis of placing too much faith in their own authority. That is to say, they do not have to use their minds to analyze the leadership problem and create an approach to solving it in terms of its intrinsic nature. Instead, they approach the problem on the basis of the authority they hold because of their control over the environment. This tack enables them to get people to follow as they wish them to in terms of the leader's power to reward or punish. Therefore, rather than think through the complex process of leadership as it really is, these essentially weak leaders merely go through the routine of exercising their authority.

Authority supports something that *often appears* to be good leadership, because people need to work and draw a paycheck in order to live in our culture. Thus, employees will indeed perform tasks mandated by their organization or by their leader because they must do so to support their own well-being. It is easy for people in authority to be misled into assuming that what they are doing to get people to follow is good leadership. It is not. It is merely the most superficial basis available to a leader seeking to engender followership. Those who operate on this basis make the assumption that they are leaders because they are the ones with the authority; they are the ones issuing the orders, and they are the ones quality-checking the work. Consequently, they tell themselves that they are the ones responsible for triggering the good flow of operations in their domain. The truth is much more complex.

To get followers to be aggressively and enthusiastically responsible for the highest possible quality of work takes a great deal more leadership skill than the "skill" that rests on "authority." True leadership skills require refined notions of what the mind is and how it operates. Leaders who lead without reexamining their mind—and their mindsets—are not capable of making those refinements.

Many of this book's concepts and premises contradict conventional wisdom. Therefore, I invite you to approach the text with an "as if" attitude. By that I mean that no matter how extreme the ideas presented may seem, try to accept them "as if" they are true, until you have finished the book and gained a new, and higher, vantage point over the society we are building. Taking an "as if" position will keep you from being locked in by your current beliefs, something that would cause you to "screen out" arguments that did not suit your beliefs.

Try to hold back from judging this book out of your current standards of "right and wrong" in the sphere of business and public policy. Instead, as you read, allow your current mindsets to be challenged through an unflinching comparison to the ideas and principles this book presents. Doing this may seem to move you into chaos. According to theories now being developed in science, creating such chaos may be exactly the first step needed to produce positive new conditions. The new point of view holds that after much time spent in building, improving, and tweaking a system toward greater stability, the system begins to close in on itself and become clogged in its operations. More of the same efforts to improve it will only make things worse. At this point, the path to real improvement, to something genuinely new and better, lies through chaos—the chaos that will arise as you plunge into the new and unknown to find a better way to create the system. This book is a call to leaders and citizens to find a path through the chaos that will lead to new and better ways to create and manage our world.[1]

---

1. For a deeper study, please see: Tom Peters, *Thriving On Chaos*, N.Y.: Lang, 1987, and Margaret Wheatley, *Leadership and the New Science*, S.F: Berrett-Koehler, 1992.

Chapter Two

THE MIND AS A PRISM
OF EXPERIENCE AND REACTION

Rule over your mind,
or else your mind will rule over you.

—Horace

WE CANNOT HAVE AN experience for which we do not have in our mind a program that transmits our energy to create it. On the other hand, the only experiences we can have in our life are those for which we have programs. We have literally millions of programs, most of which we put in place during the process of learning and growing through childhood. Basic biological programs, such as those that manage our bodily functions, are inherently built in, but we ourselves, through our mind, register into our internal computer the practical programs that create our habits and manage our decisions. As we set our programs, so will we set our perceptions of the world, and so will we set our personalities. As we shape our programs, so will those programs shape our perceptions and responses to what is in the world. Those perceptions then become the basis for our interaction with the environment.

In effect, through this process of early programing, we build our personality. In response to the consequences of our experiences we create our beliefs about who and what we are, how we must approach life in order to gain our comforts and pleasures, and what we must do to survive and avoid pain and threat. We put those "personality programs" in place while we are very young and then we automate them. Bear in mind, therefore, that people operating on automatic are running their lives according to programs selected by children.

With these programs in place by adulthood, the mind's first function is to keep us in touch with the outside world by bringing in stimuli that activate the mind. The mind's second function then is to evaluate the incoming stimuli. Its third function is to create our reaction to what we have perceived. The incoming stimuli prompt the mind to think, judge, or react in a great many ways—and those ways are *almost always* congruent with the mindsets that we have put in place through our educational, social, and moral conditioning. Our mind receives the stimuli and processes them through the learned mindsets ("programs" or "tapes"). Then, based on the products of those programs, the mind prompts us to act accordingly. What we do, therefore, will fit our programs—so long as we interact with the world with our minds on automatic and take for granted the perceptions and responses the mind creates for us.

I remember an amusing example of my mind fitting perceptions to remarks I heard during an interaction with one of my daughters when she was three or four years old. One evening I served her some mashed potatoes at the dinner table. She began to cry. I asked, "What's the matter?" She replied, "I didn't want that much." In what was probably a fairly exasperated voice I said, "Well, for heaven's sake, eat what you want and leave the rest." "No," she cried, "I didn't want that much. I wanted more." She had just reminded me that automatically in childhood, in response to its experiences, the mind begins to shape a person's perception of reality. The person then reacts to that imagined perception as if it were "real."

The result is that we end up, in fact, *inventing* much of the "out-there" reality to fit the perceptions we have put in place to screen and react to incoming stimuli. Thus, for example, if we enter a situation and "see" it as threatening, our mind will cause us to react defensively and perhaps aggressively. In turn, that defensive, aggressive behavior will cause people to incline toward being unfriendly and difficult with us, thereby creating a hostile and aggressive experience—just as we perceived it in the first place. On the other hand, had we seen the situation as friendly and acted accordingly, the environment may very well have presented itself to us as friendly and satisfying.

One of the most common, ever-present examples of how we create reality in our human interactions is the way we create relationships on the basis of our learned perceptions as to who is "good looking" or "attractive." Despite the fact that all persons are human, and anyone can have a beautiful heart and personality, if they fit our preconceptions of what is repulsive, we seldom seek them out to get to know them at a large party—unless someone activates another of our stereotypical tapes by informing us that this or that individual is rich or famous.

We program our mind in childhood and by the time we enter adulthood our mind is loaded with tapes that enable us to function in our complex world. Once these programs are in place and are working effectively, we tend to automate them and let them "run us." This spares us a good deal of effort and attention and frees us to enjoy our experience of living. As I have said, however, the nature of those tapes then shapes what we see in the real world. Most of us, however, have little understanding of the degree to which we operate on such automated tapes. As we glance out of a window at our office for example, we see cars and pedestrians moving around in disciplined, purposeful ways, observing speed limits, traffic signals, and indications displayed on street signs. Traffic and pedestrians ebb and flow in almost predictable patterns. These patterns are not at all haphazard, but are the results of social conditioning developed over many decades. The reasons the cars and pedestrians avoid contact with each other have to do with the fact that we have put in place deeply ingrained understandings and programs that govern our perceptions of what goes on around us. These programs automatically trigger our responses to the situations we face. Since we are raised in a common culture, the mindsets we put in place tend to be fairly universally shared by those around us. In other words, we end up with mindsets that are socially generalized. Therefore, as a social group, we act in fairly automated and integrated ways.

These conditioned beliefs, which translate into our ways of seeing and behaving, are developed over a considerable period of training and are stored in our mind. They are triggered automatically when a recognizable problem or situation presents itself. Before you become complacent about this process, shrug and say, "What's wrong with running on automatic?" let me remind you again that it was as an inexperienced child that you put those tapes in place. The most significant basic ones—the ones that shaped your basic personality—were installed before you were six years old, and some of the most important tapes were installed before you were three or four. Then you expanded upon their basic form until you were twelve to fourteen years of age. From then on, you added new skill and knowledge tapes—which filled out, but conformed to, the system in place.

Think for a moment about what this means: You, as an adult, are running your life on automated programs set in place by a child in response to a need to protect its being and survive in an environment not at all of the child's making. *Needed adjustments to those programs frequently do not get made— or are made inadequately—because the person simply feels safer staying with what worked when he or she was very young.* We tend to cling desperately to these programs (which form our "comfort zone") even when it has become abundantly clear that we need a new model. Whereas we are apt to turn in our used car for a new one as soon as the engine begins to falter, most of us live to our death with our original basic mindsets, even though some of our programs are outmoded and no longer provide an effective response to the realities of our changing world.

Faced with clear indications that one or another childhood tape has become inadequate, especially if the data includes pain, severe discomfort, and survival threat, we will indeed change our programs. We finally make the change because painful or frightening experiences—such as physical abuse of a wife who had sworn she would never separate from her husband—override the automation and force us to be aware of the program that is causing the problem. With that awareness, all but the most intellectually incompetent people create new programs. A boy growing up in the rural South learns to recognize and be wary of the black widow spider. Seeing such a spider crawling up his arm would immediately tap into the mindset that says "danger." Trying to remain calm (triggered by another mindset that says "Don't alarm poisonous spiders into biting"), the boy would shake or brush the spider off as best he could. However, a boy visiting the South from a region where the black widow was unknown, a boy perhaps who had been accustomed to letting harmless spiders crawl up his arm, would react differently. No program would post a danger sign and he would not be immediately concerned with getting the spider off his body—until a native with a different mindset came along to advise him of the risk. The native boy's warning effectively changes the visiting boy's programming on the spot. For future encounters with the black widow, the out-of-state boy will react just like the southern native, now that he has a new program in place.

Unfortunately for society, most of the conditions that are posing serious new threats to our well-being, and perhaps to our survival, are so complex and abstract that some of us never become aware of them. Gradually accumulating social problems creep up on us so slowly that we do not notice them until they become crises. Though the conditions that cause these crises are a direct product of the actions generated by our automated programs, we are unaware that our mindsets are the cause. So, instead of fixing ourselves, we devote our time to fixing things "out there," fixing the environment, usually resisting exactly the changes needed to remove the problem. Thus, we are quite aware that our deficit economics is posing a danger for our future, but when we set out to balance the budget, we carefully avoid "biting the bullet" by not cutting those budget items that satisfy our personal "programmed" needs. Likewise, we continue to expand the prison system to deal with crime, while avoiding the task of determining and changing the conditions that cause so many of our citizens to program their minds in ways that make crime an almost inevitable life choice.

The key to finding the courage to change is understanding that we are neither our mindsets, formed by our social conditioning, nor our minds (not as receiver or processor). We use our mind as an absolutely essential part of our daily functioning and where we store our mindsets. *But we ourselves are separate from both.* We demonstrate this (usually unconsciously) when we say such things as, "I've got a good mind to..." or ask someone, "What's on your mind?" A person "has" a mind, rather than "is" his mind. An aware person *consults* her mind. An aware person can *change* her mind.

We, or at least our leaders, must arrive at the awareness that the summation of individual automated minds results in a social mind automated in the same manner. That being so, if leaders seek to make significant social changes that call for new behaviors, they must not begin by calling for the new behavior out of old mindsets, but must first devise leadership that induces followers to get off automatic and change their minds.

Chapter Three

OPERATING YOUR MIND

We must always change, renew,
rejuvenate ourselves; otherwise, we harden.

—Goethe

We are born into life equipped with full supra-consciousness. In other words, we are totally open to, and responsive to, an aware experience of our aliveness. As we "grow up," however, we tune into outside influences that condition us to retreat from our true, fully aware selves and from our deepest awareness of our being. We begin to devote our attention to the outer world. We begin to act however we must in order to please others, or else to draw attention to ourselves and our needs. Or we try to copy others' behavior at the expense of just "being ourselves." And many other things.

As individuals create and grow their personalities, they vary the amount of consciousness they allow to surface and be experienced. These variations are created as individuals develop patterns of defensiveness to protect themselves from experiences perceived as frightening or painful. Here I am not talking only about fear of objective, external things; I'm talking about the threatening subjective beliefs and realities that are created in the minds of children as they learn to deal with the world. When their minds confront them with such frightening beliefs and realities, the fear generated is painful. They learn that these frightening and painful mind experiences can be removed by what turns out to be the process of repressing them into a state of unawareness in the unconscious mind. This process does not constitute growth but, really, regression. People move from an individual supra-consciousness or openness to perhaps a state of ego-mind-awareness, and then, later in childhood, to predominantly a state of program-awareness. At that point, they enter into a life largely based on automated mind operations.

To over simplify the idea of that regression, imagine that as a baby we accepted everyone we met unconditionally: white or black, old or young, Jew, Moslem, Christian, or Agnostic. We *the baby* sought only human warmth, smiles, attention, touch. Later, we *the child* became conscious of self as belonging to a certain category—race, religion, economic or peer group—and we began to make distinctions in our minds based on that sense of our identity. Finally, we the *adult* rigidly assumed patterns of who and what we are. If we tend to exalt our own characteristics over those of others, we create smugness or bigotry. If we denigrate ourselves and those who are like us, in comparison to others we label "superior," we engage in self-flagellation.

"Growth" for such a person would occur by recapturing that which he possessed at birth but lost or let be submerged as he created his personality with its defenses and its needs and its desires. Reemergence of early life awareness is a power-ful catalytic force for growth—opening to new possibili-ties, to higher levels of love, to trust, to tolerance, and to generosity.

STATES OF AWARENESS

Anyone who wants to change perceptions and behaviors in a manner that improves satisfaction in life must begin by resetting the source of all human behavior. That is, he must change those *mind programs* that control how he relates to the universe. If you have a mindset that tells you people find you unattractive or inadequate, even though that perception is unconscious, you will never be able to become a charismatic leader or speaker until you get rid of that mind program. If you believe that your direction of a corporate unit is invari-ably compromised because people don't think you have the courage of your convictions, your control will indeed suffer to match up to your presupposition. Just as, guess who will be bitten by a dog they encounter at a neighbor's? Exactly right—the person who is *most afraid* of dogs and most sure that a dog will turn out to be unfriendly.

Setting out to change mind programs requires recogniz-ing and dealing with three basic states of awareness.

1. Program-Awareness
2. Ego-Mind-Awareness
3. Supra-Consciousness

We all have the capacity to live our lives in any or all of these three levels of awareness. Most of us, however, are not cognizant of the three levels, in fact, are not even aware of *any* of them. Virtually all of us go through our lives taking our degree of awareness for granted. Since the level of aware-ness you are operating from, at any given moment, has a profound effect upon how you see the world and how you react to it, operating without awareness and control of these states is like being an art critic unaware that you are color blind.

These states of awareness are progressive. That is, a mind can evolve from one to the next. Also, people shift from one level of awareness to another under varying conditions in their life experience. *For one who wishes to create life from choice, it is essential that he or she become aware of the three levels of awareness, and remain aware or conscious of which level he or she is operating from at any given moment.*

The lowest level of awareness—program-awareness—is the most common in society. Ego-mind-awareness, a state that may incline either toward good or evil, is fairly common, particularly among educated individuals, but tends to be used without awareness that one is in that state, and without awareness of the nature of that state's operations. Supra-consciousness, which is our sense of God within us, inclines wholly toward what is good. It has thus far been in terribly short supply *and it is this state of mind that our world needs critically if we are to overcome the system challenges that even now jeopardize our survival.*

PROGRAM-AWARENESS

In the state of program-awareness, a person is conscious only of what existing mindsets generate from the repository of their programs. A person in program-awareness consciousness behaves largely as an automaton. This person's truths are programmed early in childhood and adolescence, as they are for everyone. The program tapes are then put on automatic and operate without further conscious choice. Faced with situations of life, the program-aware person's experience will be whatever fits the tapes. His response will be inflexible, varying only within the limits of the various tapes. If a person believes "I am my mind," then the mind will resist any effort to change the mind's programs from that which it has learned is "right." It does not matter that what it learned as right no longer fits the changing world; the ego will resist and rationalize beautifully to make the old ways appear to be sensible.

People who behave in this manner to the extreme may be seen as bigots or racists or egomaniacs. At a lesser level, they may be seen as self-righteous, stubborn, perfectionistic, or willful. At an even less pronounced level of program-awareness, certain people may be considered "well trained," "well organized," "dedicated," "conscientious," or "socially responsible." Of course, if their tapes don't fit society, they may be seen as hopelessly radical, looney, or inclined to romantic dreams, and are likely to be labeled "misfits."

Some program-aware people have strong beliefs about the nature of personal growth, about what constitutes success, or about what "really counts" in life. They are apt to slave on and on in order to see their beliefs come true, even though they are not happy, don't play, are overstressed, are jeopardizing their health and perhaps are destroying their family. They seem unable to change their behavior because change would contradict their deeply ingrained notion of self, which they usually defend automatically and without reflection.

Such a person, like many before him, came to see me for help recently. He said that he had always believed that if he worked hard, became a successful executive, and had several million dollars in the bank, he would be a happy person with a good life. Now, he said, he had it all, but he was not happy. Instead, he was depressed and lonely. He had been such a workaholic he had not created or maintained close and supportive relationships with his wife and children. He had never faced, or even become aware of, the deep beliefs that made him anxious and stressed when he was not working and pushing toward his goals of success.

After a period of intensive work in self-awareness training workshops, he came to recognize the different states of awareness that were available to him, and after a bit of training, moved up to the level of ego-self-awareness. From this level, his ego set him to the task of reprogramming his operating mind. He examined and worked to disconnect certain programs that were driving him into compulsive patterns at the cost of his pleasure and joy in life. At the same time, he deliberately added new programs toward relaxing, creating and seeking the pleasures of relationships, and defining success more in terms of experiential satisfaction than in terms of "winning the battle." After that, since he continued in his self-awareness work, he learned to open up to, or enter into, his deeper supra-consciousness, which had a far-reaching positive impact on both his personal and his professional life.

EGO-MIND-AWARENESS

As has already been suggested, ego-mind-awareness is a much more conscious (and desirable) state. A person living in this state is decidedly more "in charge" of his or her mind, and is able to choose, after ample reflection, what to believe that will result in a more effective and satisfying experiential universe. Such individuals learn the capacity to change from one viewpoint or opinion to another. Doing this is greatly facilitated, of course, when one knows of the options for the different awareness states. Those who operate out of ego-mind-awareness have greater introspective power, are freer to consider a set of facts in logical fashion and then make up their mind as to which course is best. People in the program-awareness state do not make up their mind; *their mind makes them up.*

Like the program-aware types, ego-mind-aware people also have "givens" stored in their minds as a result of their childhood and adolescent conditioning. They too spend a great deal of time operating on automatic mindsets. There is nothing wrong with this, since it is energy efficient in dealing with those parts of life that can easily be handled in an automatic fashion, such as eating, sleeping, driving a car, and performing other required functions. They are, however, able to recognize habitual mindsets as such, and say to themselves, "This is what I have always believed," or "This is what my parents always preached to me," and they can also step back from those beliefs, become more detached, and reconsider their validity in the light of current experience.

Ego-mind-aware people offer a far better hope for a realistic rethinking of many contemporary mindsets that are shaping our society, including, but not limited to, authoritarian models of leadership-followership and extreme consumerism. They may also better recognize and promote a growing impetus toward the creation of a more compassionate form of society.

Achieving this level of capacity to use the mind is a basic, though often nonspecified, purpose of higher education. For those people who achieve it (they are still in a minority among our society's business and public leaders), the mind is more often used consciously as an instrument to transform the energy of the being into the life they choose to create for themselves. They use their power to change their minds. Their awareness includes some of the inner depths of their mind, and also extends outward to take into consideration many facets of the world around them.

One quality of ego-mind-aware people that enables them to be more flexible in changing their mindsets is their willingness to tolerate being out of their "comfort zone." That is the place of safety and good feeling experienced when we stay within the bounds of our conception of *what is, and who we are.* We created comfort-zone mindsets in our early conditioning to protect ourselves, and to obtain what we wanted. Violating those boundaries triggers warnings in the form of painful emotions of fear, shame, guilt, anger, hurt, and depression. Like the electric fence that keeps cattle within the limits of a single strand of wire, the threat of these emotional pains keeps people within the bounds of simple mindsets they have placed around their own life spaces. As long as the pasture is adequate, cattle that have been conditioned to stay within the electric fence will remain penned up. Let the pasture become too poor, however, and cattle will accept the pain as they break through the fence. Survival is a very strong need. It can overcome the fears that normally keep a human —or an animal—restrained in a comfort zone.

Likewise, people, if their lives are reasonably satisfying, will stay in the comfort zone of beliefs that avoid the negative emotions they dislike. If their lives become painful and neurotic enough, however, they often become willing to leave their emotional comfort zone, to break through their controlling mindsets, and to build broader and freer life spaces. At this point, they shift from a program-aware mode to an ego-mind-aware mode, and can begin to change their minds, and therefore, their lives.

This process is central to the leaders who decide to change their mindsets as required to increase the power and effectiveness of their leadership in order to meet the growing challenges of our times. That change of leadership, of necessity, will also have to focus specifically upon the process of getting followers to change their mindsets to accord with the leader's new mindset.

I have seen this pattern of attempting to break from the limits of one's comfort zone over and over again in working with people who are trying to improve unhappy marriages. Many spouses spend years acting out mindsets that hurt or upset their partner. Since they blindly accept the "truth" of their own mindsets, their only interpretation of what is wrong between them is that a conflict is somehow the "other person's fault." The only path that will save these relationships is the path that leads them out of the comfort zone. Each must accept the discomfort of giving up old beliefs, and trading them in for mindsets that actually contradict those beliefs. Only then can they hope to create a life space that is mutually acceptable and comfortable for both of them. This is a process of moving out of program-awareness into ego-mind-awareness, and carefully creating the new mindsets and a new comfort zone.

Some people cannot take the step. I had a couple in counseling recently whom I tried to help see a pattern of action that might make the marriage viable. When I asked the husband what he thought of the plan, he was quiet for a moment, and then said, "To tell you the truth, Doctor, I'm afraid it would work." He concluded, however, that he would be unwilling to bear the emotional pain he would experience trying to give up the beliefs that he would have to violate in order to adopt the new pattern in the relationship. The extreme power of the ego to hold people within their comfort zone is exemplified in the unfortunate cases of people so

DEGREE OF SELF-CONTROL WITH RESPECT TO AWARENESS

SUPRA-CONCIOUSNESS

Person is under the influence of higher, larger forces.

EGO-MIND AWARENESS

Person selects programs by choice rather than automatically.

PROGRAM AWARENESS

Person is controlled by programs already in place and needs to ensure their correctness.

The purely human, physical, mental, self is in greatest control of one's life at the level of ego-mind awareness, under the force of self-meta-programming. Control by self decreases as one moves downward into program awareness, under the force of ego-meta-programming which forces self unconsciously to take positions which sustain mind's programs. Control also decreases as one moves upward into supra-consciousness to come under the force of essence-meta-programming. Here, higher, larger forces dictate the parameters within which the self takes positions.

trapped by their mindsets that they actually live out their lives in relationships of constant misery. Even more extreme are the cases of those who commit suicide rather than face the protracted discomfort of breaking through the boundaries.

SUPRA-CONSCIOUSNESS

Supra-consciousness or "being-consciousness"—I use these terms interchangeably—is above and beyond mind; it is the aliveness of consciousness that is the soul, or the inner being that is inhabiting the body and that manifests itself through the mind and its body. Although supra-consciousness is difficult to describe or define, it can be experienced. And when you experience it, you have a sense that it includes all other states of awareness. It is superior to them, and it makes you one with all that exists. Some just call it "the void." Supra-consciousness cannot project itself, insofar as we now know, except through the instrumentation of the mind and the body. But if it infuses the mind, it will cause the mind to direct itself differently—more compassionately and in accord with all that lives and has being, a reflection of the Divine. Whereas both program-aware and ego-mind-aware people can direct themselves either toward good or bad ends—or anything in between—those who are fully in touch with their supra-consciousness will be impelled toward the good.

This concept of our inner being was much discussed in the speculative philosophy of an early twentieth-century Florentine, Roberto Assagioli. He refers to the living conscious awareness of *"I, ness."* A program-aware person has some concept of "I", but it includes very little supra-consciousness. An ego-mind-aware person already has considerably more of that. But real enlightenment comes when we discover how to access our supra-consciousness, which is the deepest part of our selves, in full measure. We all have this state available to us, or rather we all *are* it; it's just that few of us have yet learned how to tap into this deeper part of our being. A point to understand is that the higher self-consciousness does not have the power to operate the body. It is not directly connected to the operating mechanisms. It must exercise its control and influence through its instrument, the mind. While it does not have the power to operate the body, the higher self does, ultimately, have complete power to operate the mind.

The tragedy today is that the bulk of our citizens are operating heavily out of program-awareness and few of those who lead them have yet reached the stage of supra-consciousness. We need, therefore, energetically to move humanity along the continuum from program-awareness to ego-mind-awareness to supra-consciousness, and this, I believe, we must do fairly rapidly. Otherwise we shall not be able to attain the societal consciousness we'll need to resolve the problems that are accumulating as we heighten the complexity of our society. Instead, we appear to be holding onto our traditional automated mindsets and the limited degree of leadership and followership that such mindsets are able to generate.

OBSERVING ONE'S MIND

To attain ego-mind-awareness, one must be, or become, an observer of one's mind. From a new vantage point, a person can stop "being one's mind," stop responding like a puppet to strings being pulled by automatic mindsets, and can in effect, create new mindsets. A person can do this from two perspectives. First, the ego-mind-aware person can establish a part of ego's mindset as a position of "willpower," and from that ego position can force the rest of the mind to take new positions. In this case, the individual is using ego-mind-awareness to modify his mind.

The other approach, the more fundamental and more deeply human approach, is to move from the ego-mind-aware state to the supra-conscious state of the higher self, and from there to control the reprogramming of the mind. Through a process of meditation, dialogue, and reflection, we can rise above our set programming and position ourselves at that higher level within our own consciousness. Doing this is what I term "moving into the higher self." From there we can look down upon the rows of mindset files neatly stored in our mind's consciousness. We can see that we are not they, that we are not even our mind—the repository for the mindsets. We are either ego or a being; we have both a mind and mindsets, but *"we"* are *"other."*

We will thus have achieved an *observer point of view* from outside our ego. This achievement does not come painlessly and is no small accomplishment. It usually takes a long time to practice and exercise our reflective and imaginative faculties to reach supra-consciousness.

CHANGING MINDS

Both program-aware and ego-mind-aware people typically operate automatically using fixed "programs." In both cases, people possess the capacity to change their minds. The difference between these two types is one of degree. The simple program-aware person will be much more wedded to his fixed "programs" and often will not even be aware that he or she is operating on the basis of such mindsets, and will only go against the "programs" in the face of overwhelming evidence that they are not producing desirable results. One current social example of this may be the process of slow and deliber-

EGO META–PROGRAM	SELF META–PROGRAM	ESSENCE META–PROGRAM
I am my mind.	I am not my mind.	I am one with all things.

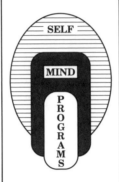

EGO META–PROGRAM	SELF META–PROGRAM	ESSENCE META–PROGRAM
Operates for the survival of the programs in place. Reality is fixed. Righteous/Bigoted Right/Wrong Win/Lose Emotions are controlling. Choices and decisions that create life are cut off from supra–consciousness and mind's free will. Subject only to ego controls, the mind's efforts to maintain its positions once it has defined its positions as "self." Mind has become ego and consciousness has become mind. Resists any new programming.	Separation of self & ego. Mind positions set by choice considering their effects on life using rational objective intention. Mind can reprogram itself on basis of awareness of changing realities/environment. Chooses programs that support the creation of life and life energies.	God consciousness. Experiences self as an expression of a greater energy or larger life force of the universe. Expresses harmony, lovingness, oneness with all people and the universe.

ate change of the social body from smoking to non-smoking in the face of accumulating evidence of smoking's frequently fatal effects. Another may be our slowly changing approach to welfare as a social institution.

The ego-mind-aware person is by definition ready to see and appreciate that she is neither her mind nor her mindsets, and that the "tapes" upon which she usually runs her life were inculcated during formative years. When presented with evidence that such tapes are ineffective for resolving a given situation, the ego-mind-aware person has far greater flexibility to reexamine the data and look at ways of installing new mindsets and proceeding in a different fashion.

LEADING CHANGE

A leader who operates out of ego-mind-awareness is in a position to help followers move out of program-awareness. He can lead followers to distinguish between responses called for by their present mindsets and the new approach proposed by the leader. In the simplest case of changing minds, a leader can encourage followers to challenge an outdated mindset and to replace it with a more supportive one that already exists in their mind's file box. I have seen this happen in a number of companies where management's mindsets produced behaviors and attitudes that caused workers to generate low morale and a good deal of anger. In these cases the leaders were largely unaware that what they were doing was having this effect. In fact, they had positive motivations and intentions with respect to workers' needs and feelings. They may have been aware of the anger and low morale, but they had no idea they were its source. All it took to improve these situations was the creation of a reliable negative feedback loop to cause the leaders to see what it was they were doing that created the negative impact. In line with their already existing intention to support workers' satisfactions, managers readily called on different mindsets to produce action that would create the impact needed to change morale and get rid of the anger. The workers already had mindsets that caused them to react positively to the leaders' changed behavior.

A much more difficult leadership challenge exists when what is needed is a change in follower behavior that is absolutely contradicted by their mindsets. Leadership in such cases must not be focused on getting the desired behaviors; it must be focused on the task of changing the followers' mindsets. A recent example is the leadership problem faced by government and health authorities in persuading tobacco companies to change their marketing strategies so they no longer target teenagers.

Chapter Four

SPIRIT

Aim above morality. Be not simply good.
Be good for something.

—Henry David Thoreau

Some readers may ask, "Why should we bother ourselves with trying to develop 'supra-consciousness' or 'supra-leadership?' Has civilization not done well enough for hundreds of generations by simply trusting unmanaged evolution? It brought us to where we are today, did it not?" Yes, it did. However, the impulses that energized man's reactions in past struggles with society-building—conquering nature, defending against enemy encroachment, questing after comfort and practicality—are no longer appropriate for resolving social problems and securing a healthy future for our planet.

Without rechanneling our energies in response to the sparks of spiritual consciousness, we are likely to founder on the shoals of erratic and antihuman development. The widening gap between the well-off and the poor, the resurgent nationalistic forces that employ genocide or massacre against those who are "different," and the listless set of minds while our planet is under assault by pollution of air, land, and sea, should force us to change our course, or else face possible cataclysmic devastation.

I have said repeatedly that you are not your mind and your mind is not you. The question arises then, "If I am not my ideas and I'm not my mind—who am I?"

At root, you are the deep "inner being," a "supra-consciousness" who makes use of your mind as a vehicle for manifesting your aliveness. Without a mind you would lack the means for transforming your "being energy" into life. Most of us get out of touch with our deep inner being, however, and focus our awareness, our sense of identity and personhood, at the level of our minds and bodies. It is easy, then, to experience that "person" as who we are. But the real "us" exists at a deeper level. Discovery and awareness of our real self is necessary to foster the growing of our soul.

If "I" is limited to our mind's awareness and if our mind is predominantly made up of our socially conditioned programming, then our actions are generally limited to what meshes with the society that shaped us. This enables us to fit in nicely, with little effort. However, this can also limit us so much that if society changes dramatically, we may find it difficult to make the changes called for by the new conditions. We may be slow to muster the energy or the solutions needed to meet the increasingly sharp challenges posed by contemporary life on the threshold of the year 2000.

If, on the other hand, "I" is experienced as a deep inner being existing at a higher level than the mind, then our mind is not free to operate without our supervision and we are able to shape and direct our mind from "supra-consciousness."

Four / Spirit

Our consciousness, what I call a being, living in a body and a mind, tends towards union with God and with all the rest of creation. At the highest level of being there is spiritual purpose. Theologians and philosophers continue a centuries-old debate on the nature of that purpose, and it is not my intention to join that debate on these pages. I hope we agree, however, that our higher inner being seeks always to respond to some call for spiritual growth, for betterment of self-realization, and for enhanced quality of life for others who share our planet. To achieve this we must change our course.

Some may ask: Cannot some of us be "excused" from focusing our attention on this project of changing course? Won't just a coterie of academics, politicians, and a few activists suffice to tip the scales in favor of our planetary society's survival?

No, none of us should beg to be "excused." In my estimation, the project of changing course is one that will require all the leadership energy we can possibly muster. Furthermore, it will require that the leadership do what is necessary to engage the major part of the population in the process of redirecting the course of social evolution. *All* of us must pitch in.

As I see it, we are sailing the ship of society without an adequate moral compass to guide our course. Such a compass consists of a mindset of conscience, an intention to adhere to a framework of ethics, compassion, and a concept of the greater good of society, mankind, and the rest of the planet. A person's intentions and actions are the products of the set of their mind. Since social mind is an amalgamation of individual minds, so too are the intentions and actions of society social organism products of those mindsets.

To this end I spoke of society as being composed of many "minds," and went on to talk about minds as the repositories for our personal, social, and spiritual "mindsets." Nonetheless, I also invited you to experience yourself as, in your essence, a deeper being that is separate from both mindsets and minds—even though many people experience themselves only as their minds (or even as merely their mindsets).

We looked at three levels of consciousness: program-awareness, the level upon which the vast majority of us appear to operate most of the time; ego-mind-awareness, the higher level from which we can look down upon our minds and our mindsets and consciously make changes; and supra-consciousness, which I described as "the aliveness of consciousness of the soul." This is that part of us which connects us to the Divine and to a fellowship with all of creation, the part of us that desires to promote what is good for the whole organismic body we call society. It will be through a process of convincing more and more people—leaders especially—to open themselves up to this level of their being that we will be able to execute the societal change of course we so critically need to make. Bringing more and more leaders into supra-conscious awareness will also help us anchor society with a clear moral compass that will be generally agreed upon throughout the leadership-element.

I am not here to recommend any particular religion or school of spirituality. Each of you has his or her own, whether you acknowledge one or not. But belonging to one or another Christian denomination, to a Jewish synagogue, or a Moslem mosque or to any other religious group does not mean that you are deeply spiritual. There are supra-conscious agnostics and program-aware evangelicals. Some children at age six have a higher level of awareness and "connectedness" than some people in their sixties who hold advanced degrees. And Americans, despite all their economic and technological prowess, are not necessarily the people best suited spiritually to map out our planetary change of course. (For one thing, Americans' intense focusing on the materialistic side of human existence is an obstacle for charting the wisest spiritual course.)

I have spent twenty-five years now working with thousands of people in self-awareness training workshops, and through that experience I have definitely moved away from a rather cynical view of the nature of humans to a clear realization that all of us possess, and live relatively close to, a deeper spiritual side of ourselves. Our routinized mindsets tend to obscure our vision of our spirituality, but that spirituality, or inner consciousness, is universally there—with all of us. Different people express that spiritual core in different ways, striking a variety of philosophical notes. But when people gather together in one place to explore their deep inner beings, the result is an agreeable chord.

Let each of you, reading what follows, draw upon the best and the highest tenets of your own belief system, realizing that, at the same time, other readers are doing the same. If you were all able to come together in one gigantic stadium or field, you would find that you have much more in common than you thought. And in articulating to each other your highest ideals and aspirations you would, inevitably, find broad streams of convergence around such notions as love, compassion, service, honesty, and generosity. You might have different names for "God" or "the Divine," but out of an ascending supra-consciousness emanating from each participant, you would be drawn together in harmony.

Something like this gathering needs to take place on our planet, even though we remain dispersed in our various cities, towns, villages, and rural areas. We urgently need a coming together in a commonality of spirit. We need shared understandings of how we can best think, plan, and act in unison with other compassionate human beings. We have reached a point in the development of society where it is becoming quite possible for us to bring about a commonality of spirit for people dispersed throughout the planet. We now have the means of communication for instant contact among peoples across a broad spectrum of languages, cultures, religions, and lifestyles. If we begin to learn to use these channels for expressing our deepest concerns, we shall be on the path to generating a more compassionate human society. And out of such united efforts we will attempt to answer the clarion call sounded by Norman Cousins as quoted in the frontispiece of this book.

THE STUNTING OF SPIRITUAL GROWTH

In many respects we have been losing spiritual power in inverse proportion to our gains in technological and economic power. The metaphor of global society as a technological giant with a mind the size of a pea, as was the case with certain gangling prehistoric creatures, is not inappropriate. And if the social mind has failed to grow at the same rate as our social body, where is our social spirit?

Early man, living closer to nature than most of us do today —which means also living closer to his own being than we now do—had a greater appreciation of phenomena such as the sun, rainfall, wind and darkness, and the inner tides of human experience. To him these elements were powerful reflections of a Divine presence. That presence now seems to escape us, huddled as we are in the shadows of skyscrapers and accustomed to all-night lighting and urban pollution that blots out the stars. We, indeed, by contrast with our ancestors, spend much of our time pursuing or maintaining the mechanistic paraphernalia of our culture, including many hours spent absorbing questionable entertainment projected from a box in our living room, bedroom, or den. (If, however, TV were not so taken up with the provision of opiates for the mind, it could become a major force for the development of a spiritual commonality.)

Before the eighteenth-century "Enlightenment," people were naturally more in touch with their nonrational intuition and more inclined to credit Providence or other supernatural forces with cycles of birth, healing, and death. Society was simpler, the human life span shorter and people were less mobile, more rooted to their region of birth. Individuals learned more readily what they needed to know to live in relative safety and comfort in their natural settings. They were, therefore, freer at an earlier age to turn toward the things of the spirit.

But we have long since moved past the stage of primitive safety and comfort—at least in first and second world nations—into a complex, demanding, and constantly changing condition we call modern civilization.

Our highly technological and materialistic culture demands ever more attention and energy from us, extending the period of "growing up" and learning until past age twenty. We still do not consider people "adults" until they are past twenty-one. And it now takes so much time to prepare to earn a living and get one's career under way that we have practically lost our awareness that there is anything more to life than making money and getting "comfortable." Neil Postman puts it trenchantly when he writes: "The success of twentieth-century technology in providing Americans with convenience, comfort, speed, hygiene, and abundance was so obvious and promising that there seemed no reason to look for any other sources of fulfillment or creativity or purpose."[1] We have tended to become so enmeshed in our material pursuits, in staying focused on the "practical things" of life that we have little room left for "being-awareness" or "supra-consciousness."

Despite the many years now that I have been leading self-awareness workshops, I still find it saddening to observe the painful cost that so many people pay for having locked their deeper selves away from expression in their daily life. They lock their deeper compassionate and joyous selves away behind so many "shoulds, musts, ought to's, got to's, and don'ts," leaving themselves with so few avenues of true self-expression. It is amazing to see, over and over again, the outpouring of hurt and grief and tears that erupts from their lost selves when people break those barriers and experience themselves as they really are. It took me years to see how truly we trap ourselves when we lose touch with our being, become our minds, and then lock ourselves into such restrictive and often self-repudiating beliefs and mindsets. These mind traps so often rob us of our spiritual domain.

Furthermore, such need for spiritual outlet or support as may remain tends to be satisfied by an aspect of culture that we have created to meet that need—organized religion. As a social substitute for "being-awareness," or spiritual attention to the life deep within us, many of us have put ritual, dogma, or a string of religious beliefs in its place and persuaded ourselves these things will satisfy our deep spiritual needs. And then we take the energy that previously was dedicated to honest spiritual pursuits and transplant it into the sphere of our professional or social life. In such a way have money, professional or amateur sports, gambling, and television become the gods of late twentieth-century life.

To ritualize people's beliefs and practices is not the intent of the churches, of course, but it is nonetheless what tends to happen. People turn their religious understandings into mindsets and set their minds on "automatic" so they won't have to spend much energy in reflection or in rethinking their commitments. We are indeed prone, perhaps out of a certain moral lassitude, to reduce spiritual experience to memorized prayers or rigid adherence to dogmas or disciplines.

We have done something quite similar in the sphere of technology, which, to a degree, has been challenging organized religion for supremacy as a place of worship. Max Frisch, a Swiss author, suggests that we may now define technology as "the knack of so arranging the world that we don't have to experience it."[2]

Notice that if we turn most of our attention outward—e.g., to observance of ritual or to participating in the "right" activities—we will consequently spend little time looking inward. The universe of our existence then becomes our body and what affects it (food, the weather, our physical surroundings, work, amusements) and our mind's preprogrammed beliefs. Since we have to transcend these things in order to experience our deep inner being, our shallow focus tends to preclude much supra-consciousness or, in religious terms, "spirituality." We thus greatly compromise President John F. Kennedy's hope that our society be remembered "not for victories or defeats in battle or in politics, but for our contribution to the human spirit."[3]

Please do not misconstrue the remarks above as an "attack" on churches. For centuries the Ten Commandments and other guiding principles taught by the churches have served as social precepts that have supported a positive social development—regardless of whatever occasional misapplications may have occurred. Without such guiding principles, and the force of the churches' authority behind them, it is doubtful that society would have evolved with the useful caveats and structure it has today. Values taught for so long by the churches have suffered in recent years, in any case, with the erosion of parenting due to divorce and the latchkey child phenomenon, scandals involving celebrated television evangelists or priests and ministers convicted of sexually abusing children, and our general succumbing to materialism as a primary objective of human life.

The Industrial Revolution indeed moved us into a world of plenty, but it also created a worldwide philosophy of materialistic indulgence. This approach to life has led us close to a rampant consumerism that is moving us toward spiritual depletion.

As we have tended to over-involve ourselves in the quest for instant gratification, our point of observation has gravitated toward the short-term rather than the long-term aspects of life. All of this results in a stunting of spiritual growth, which is part of western culture in general, and of American culture in particular. This leads to mindsets that focus on personal goals at the expense of goals promoting compassion for others and overall harmony in society. Despite a growing attention to awareness, some grounded in New Age movements and the like, which also promote greater compassion, most human minds still tend to operate at the level of program-awareness, or, at best, ego-mind-awareness, and tend to exclude supra-consciousness. This tack involves a general abandoning of social evolution to the powers of ego ("survival of the fittest"—or cleverest or, in some cases, of the least scrupulous). Ego is always selfish, as opposed to supra-consciousness, which is holistic and compassionate.

Four / Spirit

SPIRITUAL STIRRINGS

Any number of relatively recent movements have shown us that underneath the dross I have been describing there are new flames of spiritual ardor trying to break through. In some cases these are reform groups within the existing church structures that give more attention to personal prayer or meditation or hands-on social gospel projects (working with AIDs or terminal cancer patients or prisoners); in other cases they are entirely new types of religious or parareligious bodies, mind-body awareness centers, Eastern Spirituality seminars, or consciousness retreats. Some, like EST, attempt to tap into the wellsprings of power latent in each human soul, while others, like the Church of Sun Myung Moon, propose patterns of disciplined lifestyles and spiritual focus designed by a guru figure.

Some charismatic or dynamic guru types have, as we know, led followers terribly astray, as was the case with Jim Jones and the People's Temple in Guyana that ended in a mass suicide of nine hundred cultists, and as was the case of David Koresch's Branch Davidians at Waco, Texas. That such groups do rise up and attract substantial followings shows, nonetheless, that the hunger for spiritual experience is not passe. Indeed, in many American high schools, student-organized spiritual groups range from evangelical Christian cells to groups touting witchcraft or Devil worship.

Often quite healthy forms of a new spiritual consciousness in America emerge from twelve-step groups cropping up from the AA model. Such groups now aid millions to free themselves from mental and emotional prisons of dependency on alcohol or drugs or from crippling habits of "codependency" formed in reaction to living with substance-dependent persons.

[53]

Talk therapy (ranging from traditional psychoanalysis to many other models) has also mushroomed in recent years and has helped many people embark on a search for their deep inner selves. Such searches must, in all cases, be characterized as spiritual journeys, if they are done with sincerity and discipline, even if they eschew any connection with organized religion.

That there is spiritual ferment in America cannot be denied. Where it will all lead, however, is very much an open question.

SUPRA-CONSCIOUSNESS AS A SPIRITUAL PATH

What is important to understand is that the basic path out of spiritual blindness or pseudo spirituality is the path of self-awareness. This means the expanding of the consciousness of self up to the level of supra-consciousness. Roberto Assagioli talked about this process as one of moving up into the level of the higher power within each individual human being. It is at that level that we can truly connect with the Divine and perceive ourselves as part of an interdependent universe of beings, all meant to be in positive synergy with each other. Those who have made this journey upward into their higher-power self have no trouble, for instance, understanding Barry Commoner's maxim, "The first law of ecology is that everything is connected to everything."

You can go to church faithfully every week and never make this journey to supra-consciousness. Or it is possible that you may not belong to any organized religious group at all and yet discover the way to tap into your higher power. The litmus test for knowing whether you have begun to operate your being from a supra-conscious level is the way you behave toward others. Those who find their thoughts and actions mired in jealousy or plans for revenge may be sure that they have not reached supra-consciousness. Nor have those who focus most of their awareness on striving toward the materialistic and objective goals of living. Those who are willing to experience love, forgiveness, and compassion in their everyday dealings may be justified in suspecting that perhaps they have gravitated up to the level of their own being.

A certain sign of having moved closer to, if not into, one's higher power when one is a leader is the burgeoning awareness of a sense of responsibility, concern, and compassion for those one is leading. A leader who leads from compassion, aware that his or her role exists because it is essential to serve the needs of the many, will inevitably experience a sense of responsibility for the well-being of those under his stewardship.

Just what, it is fair to ask, might be the results of a society in which many individuals achieved supra-consciousness?

Aggression by one people against another, such as the Serbian assaults on Moslem and Croat enclaves in the former Yugoslavia, would virtually cease. There literally would not be the will to go to war for purposes of conquest or domination or revenge. Marital relationships would receive a tremendous boost since people would listen to each other in depth, suspend judgment, and try to do what was best for each other.

We would suddenly have a searing crisis of conscience about our responsibility for leaving millions of our fellow citizens in dank, dirty, crowded ghettoes feeding on each other's pain, hatred, and disillusionment. Consequently, we would do whatever it took to radically improve their living conditions. This would translate into tremendous gains in our battle against violent crime.

Unemployment would drop dramatically as companies came to realize that they existed for more than simply producing goods and making record profits. They would see that a substantial part of their reason for being was to provide training and jobs to those willing to learn and to work. Then we would have to provide welfare only to people who were truly unable, physically or mentally, to hold down a job.

The consequent reductions in allocations to maintain vast armed forces and police departments, to say nothing of savings in welfare and prison costs, would mean that our federal budget deficit would soon disappear. Taxes could thus be reduced instead of increased. People, in general, would have the time, energy and inclination to create a society that worked for the good of all, rather than for the promotion of the special interests of a powerful few.

Utopian as it may seem to be, such would be the state of a world where supra-consciousness reigned. We have taken a few cautious steps in this enlightened direction. But we still have far to go.

---

1. Postman, Neil, Technopoly: *The Surrender of Culture to Technology,* NY: Knopf, 1992, p. 54.
2. Frisch, Max, *Homo Faber,* tr. *Second Stop,* 1959.
3. Kennedy, President John F., inscription on the JFK Center for the Performing Arts, Washington, D.C.

Chapter Five

SOCIETY AS A LIVING ORGANISM

The obvious is that which is never seen
until someone expresses it simply.

—Kahlil Gibran

The idea of society as a whole, and the idea of nations and other organizations as "social organisms," is complex and abstract to most of us. However, accepting and taking to heart such notions are critical steps toward understanding the central role of leadership in our society, and resolving problems stemming from weak, faulty, or distorted exercise of leadership. Much of whatever works well or goes wrong in our society can be attributed mainly to one thing: what the leaders who were "in charge" of the relevant situation did, or did not do, to set policy and see that it was properly carried out. I would argue that much that leaders do that goes wrong for large organizations, or for society, comes from their failure to consider the larger whole of which their unit is a part. They stay overly focused on the immediate results that affect only their unit's performance. Many other effects of their leadership—those that impact the company as a whole, or the wider society—escape their notice.

I had worked as a consultant with businesses for only a short time before I noticed something obvious that I had been overlooking: I realized that what I did to help *one part* of an organization quite often had unexpected and unplanned for effects on *other parts* of the operation. That which made marketing more effective caused problems for manufacturing. When more efficient machines were installed in manufacturing, employee morale declined. When purchasing found sewing equipment it could buy at a much better price, downtime for maintenance went up and incentive production went down. Marketing's entrance into a new product line necessitated a change in emphasis in the Research Center, which then made it difficult for Manufacturing to get the research projects they felt they needed. When the top management team became more focused in its leadership and its demands, resistance, resentment, and other difficulties arose at the middle-management and first-line supervisory levels.

Once I paid attention, it was perfectly obvious that such effects—often negative—were predictable, and that I should take them into account in my analysis and planning. It was clear that the operation of an organization was made up of many parts producing elements that were then blended together to create the whole product or outcome. The operations of those parts *necessarily* were interdependent.

Those realities were easy to see and understand. However, as I paid even more attention to the process, I saw that the inter-unit effects mentioned above were only the tip of the iceberg. I began to see that much more subtle psychological factors were operating within and among the parts of the organization and they were having important impact on the outcome of the whole operation. I found that if a leader was perfectionistic and prone to be quick to criticize errors or deviations from the norm, the organization as a whole tended to be noncreative and noninnovative. People in such organizations typically avoided taking risks and tended to suppress bad news. It didn't take much reflection to conclude that such an effect should be expected. When, however, the perfectionistic leader was replaced with a more aggressive and flexible executive—because the organization badly needed to get out of its rut and become more competitive— I found that the people of the organization responded with much resistance, and moved very slowly in the direction called for by their new superior. They were mostly set in their habits. Innovative risktakers had long since left the unit. Who was left? Only people who needed clear direction and whose main motivation was to please management. Furthermore, practices in place stressed careful review, procedural controls, and tight feedback patterns that fostered tendencies to guard one's lines of authority and responsibility carefully.

THE PERSONALITY OF SOCIAL BODIES

I began to see that an organization had a "personality" much as does a person. It acted with a cohesiveness like that of a person. The individual who is uncertain of himself tends to behave carefully in his physical and social patterns. So does an organization that is uncertain in its leadership mindset. What the leader of one department does definitely and automatically generates positive or negative effects in other departments, and for the organization as a whole. As individuals with conflicting needs and habits tend to be frustrated, anxious, explosive, rebellious, or depressed, so too do organizations—which are basically made up of people with personalities—which have conflicts between departments or functions that generate neurotic organizational patterns in very much the same way as individuals do. Just as an individual who is bored on the job tends to be motivated to work only as much as needed to get by, so too is an entire work force with low morale. As citizens become disenchanted with what goes on in government, they lose interest in sustaining the democratic process by voting. As parents insist that all children should have the right to graduate from high school, the school system adjusts teaching methods and standards to practically guarantee graduation. As a result, even gifted students are apt to graduate with skills that make it difficult to measure up to students from Japan and Europe.

Years of following up these observations taught me that I was much more successful in helping leaders make their organizations more effective and productive when I treated the organization as if it were like a person—as if it were a dynamic living organism. I found consistently that leaders who took this view of their organizations tended to be more effective in their leadership than did those who related their thinking and actions mainly to the immediate problem at hand.

WHOLES AND PARTS

I came to see that our nation, and society as a whole, were also living, holistic organisms. This view raises serious problems for leaders who hold tightly to "national sovereignty" as a primary criterion for determining the limits of their rights to action in a world of interdependent nations. "Thinking globally while acting locally," it came home to me, is a slogan that makes eminently good sense.

In brief, I came to see society as a holistic organism, much like a human body. Both correspond to Webster's definition of an organism as: 1) A complex structure of interdependent and subordinate elements whose relations and properties are largely determined by their function in the whole, and 2) An individual being constituted to carry on the activities of life by means of organs separate in function but mutually dependent.

Each human body, including the one that is holding and reading this book, is made up of, and sustained by, its parts, and the parts cannot survive without the support of the whole. While evolving into an organism the body develops generalized organs and functions. The heart and circulatory system provide nourishment to every separate part of the human body. The brain and its nervous system manage communication from, to, and among all the parts. The immune system protects the entire person. Yes, the body can continue to function if arms, legs, or certain specific organs are damaged or lost, but none of the parts can continue if the generalized organs, such as the heart and the lungs, cease to operate.

Given a choice between actions that sustain one and destroy the other, priority must go to the survival and the well-being of the whole over the part. It is better to lose an arm than to lose one's heart or both lungs. This is obvious and taken for granted not only by doctors and surgeons but also by the patient. *It has not been obvious, however, that the same thing is true, or is rapidly becoming true, in the case of the evolving social body.*

A difficulty in dealing with society as a whole, and with nations and other organizations as a "social organism" is that the "organs," the parts of social bodies, are not as easily perceived and defined as are those of a physical human body. They consist of real but intangible elements, such as economic, political, and social systems. They include the institutions of government, the military, education, health care systems, the church, and business. Business subcomponents range from agriculture to mining to transportation to communication to manufacturing and a wide spectrum of retail and service industries.

Individual companies, and even states, might be identifiable as specific social-body organs. On the other hand, international systems of communication, transportation, health management, transnational monetary management, business and trade networks are generalized functions affecting the well-being of the whole world as a social body.

Any number of possible disruptions in those social-body parts now have the potential to injure or even destroy the social body. If the human body falters in the production of white and red blood cells, there is no way to provide adequate support to the cells and organs. If society's educational institution fails to supply needed technicians to keep our production and service systems in operation, there will be no way to meet society's material needs. Just as a collapse of the body's circulatory system makes it impossible to service the needs of the body's many parts, so will a breakdown of transportation systems make it impossible to feed our populations. If the body's brain fails, the body can no longer function; the same is true if a corporation's administrative system breaks down. If the body's immune system ceases to operate, the rest of the body cannot protect itself from the ravages of the millions of microorganisms that cause disease. Similarly, if society's medical system fails, we may face sweeping epidemics of diseases that are now being held in check.

The educated public is only beginning to perceive society as a functional whole that spans the entire planet—a whole composed of millions of highly diverse but subtlety interlocking parts. Most of us still act as if society is made up simply of many individual units doing their own thing, independent sovereign states, regions, cities, companies, and local governmental bodies serving their own interests.

Paradoxically, we are most apt to treat society as an organism in regard to interdependencies of the lowest significance for our survival. We do a reasonably good job of cooperating to support the Olympic Games, for instance. But we do not cooperate well when interdependency appears to threaten the status quo. Just consider the reluctance of many manufacturers to cut pollution coming from their factory smokestacks, and of consumers' resistance to paying higher prices for related products in order to clean up the air that millions of people breathe. There is even data that suggest that industries sometimes suppress a new product, a breakthrough of some kind, because society as an organism seems to be a good idea up to the point where such support may require some individuals to sacrifice their personal interests.

However, global society has emerging purposes above and beyond the purposes of its subunits, such as the United States or Brazil. One basic purpose, as with any living organism, is survival. A normal human being has a strong need to survive, and, given the choice, most people will give the need to survive priority over the needs of any part of the body. The social organism, made up of people, also has a need to survive. However, we are just now awakening to conditions that threaten its survival as an entity, and perhaps the survival of the human species as well.

THE AWAKENING OF SOCIAL MIND

We can see a prime example of this in dealing with our ecosystem. Until recently, individuals, companies, and nations acted aggressively to meet their own immediate needs with little or no regard for the effect of their actions on the atmosphere, topsoil, animal species, the earth's water systems, or the depletion of nonrenewable natural resources. Of late, however, we see a growing concern for taking protective actions with regard to the planet and its ecosystems. Recently we applied severe sanctions against units of global society that were decimating the elephant species for its ivory. It has slowly become a given that actions that add to nuclear pollution and fallout, such as experienced by most of Europe after the failure of the Chernobyl power plant in Russia, are unacceptable. There have also been strong campaigns against the economic interests that were eroding the ozone layer through use of aerosol sprays, and destroying the tropical rain forests through over cutting. We have indeed been coming to grips with the hard facts that we must maintain the ozone layer to keep from being burned to a crisp by the ultraviolet rays of the sun, and that we need the rain forests because they generate so much oxygen for the whole planet and support so many forms of plant and animal life. In this regard we might credit here a startling statement by the naturalist Thomas Berry: "Survival in the future will likely depend more on our learning from the (American) Indian than the Indian's learning from us. In some ultimate sense we need their mythic capacity for relating to this continent more than they need our capacity for mechanistic exploitation of the continent."[1] Individual operators and companies are increasingly limited in their incursions into ecologically sensitive areas. More and tougher laws now mandate conservation practices in mining, forestry, farming, hunting, and other sectors. In these and many other ways society has begun to restrict the functioning of its subunits to support the well-being of the whole.

In other areas, too, there are indications of dramatic change. Virtually all armed confrontations between or among nations in the history of the world had to do with attempts to conquer territory or treasure—or else repulse an aggressor seeking unjust conquest—until the humanitarian operation in Somalia in 1993. Under the aegis of the United Nations, U.S. and other troops invaded a sovereign country with the sole purpose of halting internecine warfare among different bands of marauders who were, in effect, preventing food supplies from reaching millions of starving citizens. In Somalia, for the first time, troops from other nations risked their lives to confiscate arms and shut down an internal conflict purely for humanitarian reasons. This was something startlingly new in human history—an indication of just how much global consciousness is growing and of how much we are now persuaded that evil left unchecked anywhere will affect us all.

The joint military action in Iraq was an even more meaningful sign of evolving awareness. The action was made possible in large part by the assembling by President George Bush of an astonishing coalition of nations to take back the State of Kuwait from the tyrannical grip of Saddam Hussein of Iraq. Here too something quite new was at work. Arab forces from Syria, Egypt, and Saudi Arabia joined with U.S., British, Canadian, French, and Italian units, under U.S. command, to dislodge the heavily dug-in Iraqi troops who were occupying Kuwait and holding Kuwaitis hostage.

The trend evident in the actions in Kuwait and Somalia has been extended in multilateral actions taken to pressure Serbian, Croatian, and Muslim forces in former Yugoslavia to desist from war and resolve their differences in a civilized manner. The above actions indicate society's increasing understanding of itself as a holistic organism. They also point up the growing effectiveness of what President Bush termed "a new world order." This term, and the cooperation among nations that brought it into being, relates to global society's self-awareness as a holistic organism. And this is something leaders will need to respect in their thinking and acting in order to create a harmonious society.

Other signs of holistic movement can be seen on the diplomatic front. We have had an increasing number of what can be called "summit meetings" to deal with crises and problems on the world scene. There are increased efforts to establish agreements on international trade, and on monetary and ecological policies, as it becomes clearer every day that self-serving practices of one or more countries can severely upset the economic well-being of other nations, or perhaps of the world economy as a whole. The complex network of production and distribution that supplies our food and other necessities and tools of living is now worldwide in scale.

Very few places remain on the planet that can call themselves self-sustaining. The United States and the former U.S.S.R., to take just one example, long operated as military adversaries, but even so, during much of that time, Russia and her satellites got a great deal of food from U.S. stores. Now, with the dissolution of the former Communist empire, it is in the self-interest of the United States, and indeed of the whole world, that prosperous, stable nations help the remnants of the U.S.S.R. avoid social breakdown and become productive in their transition from dictatorship to democracy.

Crime that breaks out in the social body spreads like an infection throughout wider society, causing pain and debilitation. The international drug traffic is an outstanding example of such a plague. Every country has its own police forces to curtail the infection of crime. But more than that, police forces, through Interpol and other networks, have become increasingly adept in cooperating across frontiers to track down criminals and extradite them for trial. Intelligence services of various countries also collaborate in many sectors, such as in the war against terrorism. In these efforts, too, we can see evidence of our recognition of the organismic nature of planetary society.

Other signs are the growth of world banking, courts of international law, and joint efforts at controlling disease worldwide, especially epidemics such as AIDS. More and more nations, through the United Nations and through other bodies, are pooling their ideas, energy, and resources to deal with problems that extend beyond their borders. There is, unmistakably, a steady movement toward the formation of permanent supra-national councils to manage society's life systems across what were formerly sovereign borders.

Inside various nations—which are themselves simply smaller versions of world society—supra-leadership forces and practices (a concept explored in detail in chapter eight) are also on the upswing. Education systems, critical for turning out needed technicians, mechanics, engineers, scientists, economists, teachers, doctors, lawyers, and others, are subject to increasing evaluation, control, and support from governments. In the interest of the larger social good, industries are not allowed to strike in wartime, and railroads are not allowed to strike to cut off supplies to societies dependent upon their delivery. Airline controllers who decided to strike during the Reagan years were fired and replaced rather than allowed to disrupt airline services. Government employees, in general, are also forbidden from striking because society would bog down too much if government services were halted. Doctors are no longer free to design the kind and quality of their training; farmers may no longer spray DDT on their fields. The FDA strictly monitors the release of new pharmaceutical products onto the market. The consumer protection movement has spawned numerous class-action suits, which have led to decisions to hold manufacturers responsible for damages their products cause.

All these examples, and many more, demonstrate the growth of consciousness that regards society as a whole, as an entity whose health and well-being must be protected over and above the interests of individual parts. These trends are hopeful signs that society may be ready to appreciate the need for and support supra-leadership.

However, though the emergence of a self-conscious society is well under way, it is far from complete. In fact, there are as many negative signs waving like red flags as there are positive and encouraging signs. *People, governments, public bodies, companies, and individual leaders still exhibit a strong tendency to seek their own gain regardless of cost to society at large.* This is to be expected, of course, since it is often debatable which of a set of alternatives is most supportive of the greater good. And quite often what may be good for the whole will be damaging to the part. This phenomenon is what Robert Wiebe has termed "a society of segments, each presuming autonomy in its domain, each requiring homogeneity in its membership, and each demanding the right to fulfill its destiny without interference."[2] Campaigns to stop American youth from smoking will be good for their health if successful, and indeed for holding in check insurance rates and limiting the burden on our health care system of future lung cancer and emphysema patients. These campaigns will be "bad" however, for the economies of states such as Virginia and North Carolina that have depended heavily on tobacco farming and cigarette production. Likewise, the many stockholders who have tied up assets in tobacco company stock may rally against efforts to reduce smoking. A growing emphasis on controlling acquisition of firearms by the general populace may be good for the reduction of the homicide rate, but it is seen as bad by those who seek to safeguard second amendment rights to possess weapons. The setting of national standards for what shall be taught in schools may lead to higher achievement scores by high-school seniors on the SAT and other tests, but it may cripple the creativity of some innovative teachers. And so forth.

A living organism is made up of hierarchies of subsystems existing one within another. Each subsystem is a whole made up of many parts. Chemists demonstrate how subatomic units are wholes that combine to form atoms, which are again wholes that combine to form molecules, which in turn are wholes that combine to form cells. Scientists study the process by which whole cells combine to forms organs, which, as wholes, combine to form a person.

Sociologists take over from there and teach us that persons are wholes that combine to form a family, which, another whole, becomes part of a community. Communities join together to form a country or state or region, and these last, taken all together form a nation. Political scientists finish the chain by showing us how the many individual nations, inevitably, whether they want to or not, whether they are aware of it or not, form the community of nations we call "the world."

Each element, simultaneously a part of a whole and also an individual entity in its own right, has a dual task. It must meet its own needs, and at the same time, it must meet the needs of the larger system upon which it is dependent for its survival. In other words, each whole acting as a part operates within the context of contradictory demands. It must assert itself to be an effective whole, but do so in a manner required to sustain the larger whole. A police officer who chooses to risk his life in the line of duty, perhaps engaging in a gun battle with a homicidal maniac, subordinates his own need to survive as a person to the need to protect the wider society— thousands of local citizens—from the menace posed by the gunman. But these are courageous choices—which are never easy.

The social organism, like all living structures, exists in the context of such contradictory demands. Powerful *inherent* forces are constantly in tension in the struggle to achieve a balance between the poles of the self-interest, or independence, of a part, and accommodation to the demands of the larger whole. The ideal point of balance is not fixed, but shifts constantly in response to changing conditions. Since the universe is in a state of flux, a healthy organism does not assume a fixed balance, but rather remains open and ready to adjust in response to the ebb and flow of exterior influences. Thus we have long witnessed the constant shifting balance between conservative and liberal forces in our political system, and between the needs of the state as overall guarantor of our rights and the freedom of individual citizens. *Only by remaining flexible and being ready to move a bit to the left or a bit to the right, all the while allowing for a maximum of freedom of expression by those on the extremes, can a nation make adjustments appropriate to changing circumstances.*

Yin And Yang

The Chinese concepts of yin and yang apply to the two aspects of this force inherent in all living systems. Yin behavior is attuned, adaptive to the environment, cooperative, and

intuitive. Yang behaviors are aggressive, competitive, ego assertive, rational, and logical. Yang behaviors tend to be ego
based, to express the seeking and assertiveness of the individual, who is but a part of a larger system. Yin behavior is
attuned and adjusted to the larger whole. Yin seeks to blend
supportively; yang seeks to dominate and control.

So-called "primitive" groups, such as Australian aborigines,
Eskimos, and Native Americans, have tended naturally toward
yin behavior, at least with regard to nature. Our modern
Western, so-called "civilized" culture has tended toward competitive, domineering, controlling behaviors. Yang forces push
us to drill for oil wherever it may be found; yin forces seek to
balance the search for oil against the need to preserve the
environment.

Energies of the universe flow in constant interplay, a process of cosmic change. These energy flows seem to have as
their purpose the establishment of harmony, of balance.
Change is a natural condition of the universe, and, therefore, a natural aspect of every subsystem. The relationship of
parts to wholes, and of wholes to parts, is in constant flux to
maintain the synergistic quality of the system. This may entail an increase of yang energy of one part asserting its integrity, or, in another moment, a yin adaptation to needs of the
whole. There must be a certain free flow of both yin and
yang energies, a flow that will support the whole over the
part or the part over the whole.

When yin and yang are in balance, there is a mutually dependent and beneficial—synergistic—relationship between
parts and the whole. The needs of neither the parts nor the
whole have precedence over the other. Unless the synergistic balance is broken so that the integrity of either the whole
or a part is threatened, either is free to act and create and

change in its own way. If it were otherwise, the flow of evolutionary change would not be possible.

The part may act to create new conditions that expand its powers, and perhaps those of the whole as well. This may entail a period of yang behavior by the part as it imposes positive change upon other parts, or upon the entire system. The American Revolution and the Colonists' movement toward the rights and freedom of individuals, and away from subservience to a remote power that was unsympathetic to their needs, is a good example of yang behavior by a part. So too is the constant independent thrust of science in the midst of what would otherwise be a more stagnant society. On the other hand, protection of the integrity of the whole may require supportive yin behavior from the parts if the whole is to survive. Our clear need to limit industrial pollutants of air and water is a case in point.

When yin and yang forces flow freely back and forth around the point of harmony and balance, we move naturally to a state of maximum freedom for all. Conflicting conditions are not seen as win/lose, right/wrong contests, but as opportunities for creative synthesis. In that state, part/whole synergy is at its full capacity. In the long-run process of the cosmos, the flow of yin/yang energies around the least energy balance point is probably inexorable. In nonliving systems the flow is automatic, with shifts occurring relatively quickly after an imbalance develops. If, for example, moisture in the atmosphere is rendered excessive by a change in temperature, water precipitates out until balance is achieved.

As one scientist-philosopher once remarked, however, "Man is the only disorderly element in an otherwise orderly universe." Yes, man has intelligence that provides him with power to interfere with natural processes, at least within the realm of social systems, and swim—probably to our detriment—against the current. Asserting ego through intelligence has resulted in a prolonged expression of yang energies as man has sought to dominate, control, shape, and consume the environment to meet what he presumed were his personal needs. His ego, blinding him to the insignificance of his power in the face of the cosmos, has led him to act as if the universe were his to shape according to his own superficial notions and for the sake of ephemeral pleasures.

The resulting yang imbalance has brought the environment much more under our control than was the case in the natural state of things. This control, however, is more apparent than real. This is so because sooner or later the synergistic imbalance created by man's giving free rein to an imperious ego will inevitably bring forth counterforces. If, indeed, nations and private units continue to strip and consume the planet's resources in such heedless fashion, we will find ourselves forced into a yin-like adaptation that may require sharp sacrifices. If, for example, we continue to explode our population, we will be forced to limit our growth, either by Big-Brother-like crackdowns on procreation, or by the disaster of massive starvation or something equally terrible.

A Growing Need For Supra-Leadership

As we have seen in the breakdown of the Communist bloc, organizations and nations created under strong, centralized, sometimes totalitarian, controls have been sharply corrected by wars and local rebellions, or by massive social resistance to their programs, or simply by the social atrophy of peoples' will to respond and create.

If we continue to impose the products of our technology on the planet's surface, waters, and atmosphere, we may soon be brought into balance quite brusquely by excessive carbon dioxide, acid rains, or other pollutants in lethal accumulations. Such substances are capable of altering our climates, destroying our oxygen-producing forests or rendering our topsoils barren. In the more colorful expression of Mohandas Gandhi, "In losing the spinning wheel, we have lost our left lung. We are, therefore, suffering from galloping consumption."[3]

Leadership/Supra Leadership Relationship

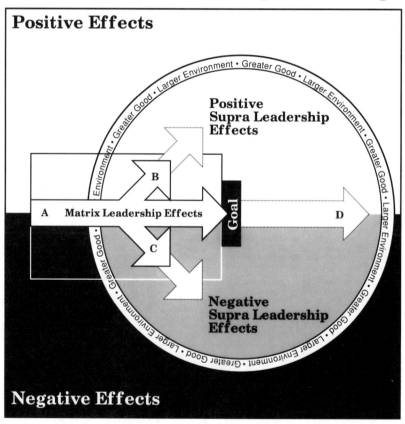

And if we continue to subordinate the needs of the human mind, personality, and spirit to the endless demands of robotizing technology, hierarchy-building and self-defending government, the idols of "business success," military "superiority," endless growth in productivity, and cutthroat competition, we may have to pay a heavy price. As Michael Harrington has written: "If there is technological advance without social advance, there is, almost automatically, an increase in human misery, in impoverishment."[4] The price will include increased demands for escapism in the form of drug abuse, crime, mental illness, and physical degeneration, which, combined, will exact a fearsome toll upon our social organism.

The need for moderation and balance is relatively clear in the case of the human organism, made up, as it is, of unique organs that, as parts, support the whole and which cannot survive unless the whole survives. If one ignores the needs of his body, under- or overeats, overindulges in drugs, alcohol, food preservatives and other additives, eats too much fat or carbohydrates, breathes too much polluted air, or fails to exercise or get enough rest, the body will suffer the consequences. Such excesses will cause the breakdown of various organs through cancer, heart disease, liver impairment, or other life-threatening phenomena.

As obvious as the consequences of these imbalances are, it is amazingly difficult for doctors, nurses, and health educators to persuade people to stop feeding their egos and start taking proper care of their bodies. It is not surprising, therefore, that the problem of persuasion is much tougher when it comes to our social habits and their net impact on our social body.

The parts of the social body are much less specific in function than are those of the human body—and not so easy to identify. Some parts of the social organism have acquired more power to exist with or without reference to the larger social body than is the case for human organs. Portions of society—groups, associations, communities, ethnic divisions—have minds of their own that, though they are part of the whole, also believe they can exist independent from the whole. Individuals and social units also have egos that are sometimes overbearing and mindlessly self-serving.

These factors create the ideal contest for the development of self-seeking, competitive, assertive yang forces among the parts of society, with each part overemphasizing its own importance and underestimating the impact of its actions upon the whole of society. Leaders of parts of society, whether those parts be nations, government bureaucracies, armies, school systems, or corporations, tend to be driven by their yang biases. They thus incline to set their goals and policies, and carry out their operations, from the yang perspective. They often regard yin tendencies as counterproductive to their efforts. Companies, for example, that bend over backward to protect the environment risk being pushed out of the market by costs that are much higher than those of less-socially aware competitors.

On the positive side, however, every excess tends to generate its counterreaction. It may well be true—and there are signs that it is—that society's yin forces are gaining in strength, moving us all toward a gentler and more compassionate world.

To achieve such a world, nonetheless, we need to recognize and promote the healthy currents at work in our society, and resist and turn back those that jeopardize our survival. This will take education, conviction and courage beyond what both our leaders and our followers have been demonstrating thus far in the twilight of our century.

1. Berry, Thomas, *The Dream of the Earth,* SF: Sierra Club Books, 1988, p. 1990.

2. Wiebe, Robert, "The Segmented Society," from the collection *Individualism in American Life,* Robert Bellah et al. NY; Perennial Library, 1987.

3. Gandhi, Mohandas, "Young India" speech, 13 October, 1921

4. Harrington, Michael, *The Other America,* Appendix, sct.1, 1962.

Chapter Six

THE NERVOUS SYSTEM OF THE SOCIAL BODY

*Mankind has become so much one family
that we cannot insure our own prosperity
except by insuring that of everybody else.*

—Bertrand Russell

The communication network of the social body is analogous to the mind, nervous system, and sensory system of the human body. If we want to understand and manage society as a social organism, we need to know how those systems work, and manage them accordingly. The human body evolves out of genes into its given form; the social body doesn't evolve out of genes; it comes out of our own thinking, leadership, and human behaviors. Since it does not have the guidance of genes, we need to know what we're doing in order to construct a healthy social body.

Treating society as a living social body with a social mind requires that we understand and deal with a process essential to, and inherent in, every complex living organism. That is, their functioning always hinges on an information network.

A flow of information and a system for handling it is a fundamental necessity for any complex organism that lives in, and interacts with, the world.

If the human body with its many parts is to function as an entity, there must be a flow of information to the mind that enables it to unify the actions of those parts in support of the integrity of the whole. There must also be a flow of information that enables the person as a whole to interact with, and deal with, the environment. A man who drinks enough whiskey to disrupt his body's internal information system loses the ability to coordinate its parts well enough to walk. And a social body that indulges in too much materialism can similarly lose its ability to operate in balance. A person who loses his senses of hearing and seeing will have trouble crossing a traffic-filled street. Likewise, a company that loses sight of major changes in the marketplace will have difficulty staying alive in business.

The requirement for information processing systems applies as fully in the social body and mind as it does in the human body and mind. The social organism must have the needed flow of information to enable it to get all of its parts to work together as an entity, and to deal holistically with the environment. Let us look more closely at how the system works in an individual as a basis for getting a better picture of how it works in a social organism.

FOUR KEY SYSTEMS

For the individual human being to function, the mind must be served by four essential communication systems.

> 1. It needs internal sensors and communication links that convey information to the mind about what is going on in all parts of the body.

2. It also has to have sensors to detect external conditions and a means of receiving data about what is going on in the environment outside the body.

3. Next, it must have a memory bank of stored data about past experiences that can be related to any given present-moment situation.

4. Finally, the mind must have the means and the power to transmit action commands to all parts of the body.

The nervous system of a human body is a fabulous communications network, instantly conveying information throughout the body to and from the brain and its internal and external sensors. The very slight sensation of a spider crawling on my foot enables my mind to initiate a total body response that saves me from being bitten. Without such a capacity, the body could not signal to the brain a lack of water, a need for food, or information about a spreading infection. Neither could the mind set in motion the myriad adjustments necessary to keep the body in balance and adapted to the complex demands of the environment.

RECEPTION OF EXTERNAL STIMULI

While it does not yet match the effectiveness of the human body's system, the social body's nervous system has already developed a high level of sophistication and sensitivity. External stimuli enter the consciousness of the social body through its eyes and ears—newspapers, magazines, TV, and radio networks. These antennae are augmented by many intelligence gathering agencies—police, FBI, Internal Revenue, Center for Disease Control, agriculture extension agents, and numerous scientific data collecting agencies.

Interconnectedness of all parts of the body is another simi-
larity between the human and the social bodies. Every part
of my body is connected to the awareness centers of my mind.
Most of the time, however, if nothing is amiss, nothing is reg-
istered. My feet and my back are all part of the network, but
unless something hurts in one of those parts, I tend to be
unaware of them. No news is good news. Let a bee sting my
back or foot, however, and my attention will be immediately
directed to that part of my body.

If all is normal in Athens, nothing about the Greek capital
will appear on *World News Tonight*. But if terrorists blow up
an airplane on the tarmac of the Athens Airport, it will instantly be news on all the world's TV and radio news programs, and it will make the front page of all the world's
newspapers. Alarmed over the terrorist activity, many people
in many different countries will cancel their travel plans to
Greece. And security will immediately be tightened at air-
ports from Nairobi to Boston to Tokyo.

This makes perfect sense from the viewpoint of society as
a social organism. Survival of any organism requires that it
receive instant demands for attention from any part of the
body that may be suffering from damage or pain. The hurt
itself will be picked up by the social body's nervous system,
which will carry the signal rapidly to the brain. Similarly, the
social body's nervous system, news reporting over various
media and person-to-person transmissions, will alert the social mind to the danger.

The mind—the leadership-element—registers such information and makes decisions to reinforce security in each lo-
cale, thus boosting the chances that the social body will not
experience additional trauma. Elements of the social mind
put in place sophisticated social programs to cope with the

damage already done and to prevent damage from spreading. Such actions tend to unify all parts of the social body in reaction to the negative event, moving global society closer together in its functioning, and more clearly into a holistic mode of operating. Thus far this mode is far less developed and less sophisticated in the social body than it is in the individual human body, but it is indeed evolving.

Our social responsiveness to problems affecting large systems, national and global, is still fairly crude, however. Society typically waits far too long before conceptualizing and applying holistic solutions to such social problems as gaping deficiencies in our educational system (allowing virtual illiterates to "graduate" from high school for instance).

From time to time the public, or certain social critics, lambast the press for zeroing in on negative news—crime, scandals, tragedies, and so forth—while soft-pedaling upbeat or positive news. The press, however, is only carrying out its role as an antenna sensitive to what has gone awry in the social body, sending signals to the mind, the leadership-element —and another part of the body, the followers—that something is hurting or broken and needs attention. The press, through its public opinion polling and through its interviews to get reactions to problems or sore spots in the social body, heightens the sense of urgency that something must be adjusted or fixed—security measures, judicial processes, or whatever, to alleviate a social ill. Without such negative feedback, little would be changed. When western observers poured into Rumania after the overthrow of the dictator Ceausescu in 1991, they found whole towns and even regions black with soot and other terrible effects of unmitigated industrial pollution. The Rumanian people, never receiving any negative feedback from a tightly controlled press, had not realized how poor and inhuman were the conditions under which they were going about their lives.

With the spread of satellite communication around the globe, bringing CNN and the BBC into living rooms and kitchens in even remote places, a phenomenon such as the news blackout in Rumania is more and more unlikely. Paul Kennedy comments:

> In a world with more than 600 million television sets, viewers are as much consumers of news and ideas as they are of commercial goods. Thus governments of authoritarian states find it increasingly difficult to keep their people in ignorance. Chernobyl was swiftly photographed by a French commercial satellite, and then transmitted all over the world—including within the Soviet Union itself. The Chinese government's suppression of the students in Tianamen Square and the outside world's shock at that were immediately reported back into China.... Just as television in the 1960s helped to shape American public perception and policy concerning civil rights and the Vietnam War, so the spread of the same technology around the world is leading to similar transformations of values.[1]

Without continuous press coverage of the starving masses in Somalia, it is doubtful that world reaction would have grown so intense that the United States and other western nations would have sent in troops to combat the feuding clans that were choking off the delivery of food. Even more dramatic was the incredibly intimate and detailed television coverage of the Persian Gulf Crisis. For the first time in history, viewers worldwide were able to have ringside seats at live bombing missions and assaults by ground troops. One consequence was a crystallizing of the social perception of war. What direction that social perception may take is not yet clear, but it is likely that more and more people will militate for an end to aggression and plundering of any one nation against any other.

Various elements in the social body's nervous systems bring information about key trouble spots before assemblies at the United Nations. Here representatives of many nations debate the issues involved and attempt to reach consensus so as to bring pressure to bear toward resolution of this or that problem. This, it should now be easy to imagine, is entirely comparable to the way blood is rushed to a hurt or sick part of the human body after the brain has received the proper information from the nervous system.

GENERATING AND ACCESSING DATA

The generation of scientific data through research and the dissemination of findings and conclusions through both specialist and generalist media are yet other facets of the social nervous system. Without the generation and dispatching of such data, we would never have been alerted, for example, to the need for action to discover the causes of acid rain, and to neutralize this harmful phenomenon. Listen to Margaret Wheatley on this subject:

> *For a system to remain alive, for the universe to move onward, information must be continually generated. If there is nothing new, or if the information that exists merely confirms what is, then the result will be death. Isolated systems wind down and decay, victims of the laws of entropy. The fuel of life is new information—novelty—ordered into new structures. We need to have information coursing through our systems, disturbing the peace, imbuing everything it touches with new life.*[2]

There is encouraging evidence, then, that the world is well on its way toward refining the complex peripheral nervous system network that it needs in order for the social mind, especially the leadership-element, to perform its homeostatic and directional functions for the social body. One heartening advance has been the awakening of the public and its leaders to the dangers of haphazard television fare, rife, for example with violence or perversion, for the shaping of society's morals.

To some extent, however, the yang needs of the news media to seek attention—since more attention means more viewers, listeners, readers, and money—lead to hype and exaggeration and this can be jarring and disruptive. In the human body fear or anger mechanisms respond strongly to negative feedback. This has survival value. However, when such pressure is constant, it produces anxiety, hypochondria, high blood pressure, and unduly angry responses to life. If someone's feedback system constantly cries wolf, alerting the person's defense systems, the likely result will be neurosis.

In the social body there is also a strong response to negative feedback.

Therefore, many of our media outlets tend to "cry wolf" as often as possible. Bad news gets attention. Perhaps we made a mistake when we tied the media—a major part of the social body's feedback system—to making money. At times almost all media outlets exhibit a tendency to exaggerate, causing an effect comparable to what might happen to a person if his feedback system made him feel more successful and important each time he hiked the negative input into his system. The people in our social body do not yet seem to have developed the self-control and sophistication needed to stop devouring exaggerated negative news.

Tapping Into Memory Banks

The social nervous system contains the third requirement for internal communication in its memory banks of stored experiences and discoveries. In vast libraries and data banks man has recorded almost everything ever learned in any part of the world, in any epoch of history. We also have greatly expanded storage of knowledge in millions of highly trained individual minds of the world's professionals. The explosive development of computers and computer networks is yet another step in the evolution of the social nervous system. All the data and understandings of many generations and cultures are now at our fingertips and can be called into play in problem-solving efforts.

Transmitting Action Commands—A Weak Spot

The fourth requirement for directional control by the social mind is the means of transmitting thought-out, conscious, and deliberate action commands throughout the body. It is in this area that our social mind is still most lacking. We have not yet achieved, on a global scale, the level of mind operation that is optimum for properly digesting available information and sending out effective signals for appropriate change in activity throughout the social body. We still fall short of producing a healthy, unified response to problems that must be dealt with at the level of planetary systems, rather than at the level of just one or another part. It is in this regard that we continue to be somewhat disorganized and spastic in our behavior as a social organism.

Even so, evidence shows that we are moving in the right direction. There are increasing contacts among diplomats and experts in a wide variety of specialities across national boundaries. We are at our best in this arena when the threat is military, such as the aggressive actions of Germany and Japan during World War II and of Saddam Hussein during the Persian Gulf Crisis. We are much more sluggish in response to threats such as pollution of the seas or depletion of the forests—though the consequences of our slackness in these areas may well rival those of terrible military aggression or rampant terrorism. The counsel of the late Vice President Hubert Humphrey is germane: "The essence of statesmanship is not a rigid adherence to the past, but a prudent and probing concern for the future."[3]

MINDSETS MOLD MESSAGE RECEPTION

It must be remembered that whatever is received, felt, or transmitted, or whatever instructions are sent to a part of the body, will be interpreted according to the receiver's mindsets that are currently in operation. The social mind is very much like an individual mind; it is programmed, in many complex ways, to receive and process certain signals and to respond in certain predetermined patterns. People, societal units, even whole cultures, *can only receive messages on channels they have opened*; thus areas of prejudice or ignorance effectively block reception of communications that do not mesh with existing mindsets. In this spirit the feedback that the Serbs received regarding their ethnic cleansing actions either fell on deaf ears, or was strongly rejected, until massive bombing damage by NATO warplanes broke through the Serbs' denial of the evil reality they had been perpetrating.

A person whose self-image is of being unattractive or unworthy will not be able to accept compliments, and will, for instance, persuade himself that a compliment was not meant sincerely or is just a manipulative technique. If we think someone does not like us, we will act distant and unfriendly toward that person and probably produce in the other a similar aloofness (which is what we told ourselves we would get from him or her if we tried to become friendly). These are examples of mindset traps.

The same sort of dynamics is at work in the social mind. An obvious example of such a mindset trap was the cold-war relationship between the former Soviet Union and the United States. Each nation conceived of the other as a terrible menace. Each then created an immense stockpile of nuclear arms, aimed them at the other and shaped interactions to counter the warlike threat of the other nation's armaments. This went on for decades.

"National security," Paul Kennedy reminds us, "(has been) used to justify almost everything from building a highway system to providing science and technology scholarships." Even in time of peace, such as in the wake of the Persian Gulf War, "national security experts and Pentagon officials can still find many potential threats to international stability—and grounds for maintaining large defense forces."[4]

On another plane, if too many of the world's peoples have the notion of the seas as boundless bodies of water quite impervious to what we dump into them, we will blithely fill the seas with pollutants until we destroy them and ourselves in the process. Likewise, even though there has been almost a ninety percent drop in some fish populations, we continue to allow intensive fishing.

Mindset traps are baited by ego, or "pride," in the negative sense of that word. Each cultural mindset operates to make certain its programs are "right." Remember that ego almost always defends against any notion of being "wrong."

QUANDARIES OF CONSUMERISM

One perhaps less than obvious mindset trap may be implicit in our first world consumerism. Early in the industrial revolution we learned that increasing materialism increased comfort, pleasure, and survival probabilities. Out of generations of such experience we have created the perception that "having and consuming more" will make us "happy." We have made this belief a cornerstone of our culture, of our "way of life," and are heavily committed to the production and consumption of material goods. When carried to the extreme we end up with gadgets such as the electric toothbrush that are totally unnecessary. We have been hard put to notice that beyond a certain point our ceaseless consuming of things has not made us one bit happier or healthier. In fact, our extreme indulgence in consumption has almost certainly been bad for our physical, emotional, and spiritual health and has been diverting us from the deeper satisfactions that life has to offer.

Nonetheless, despite the obvious evidence that we have been squandering our diminishing natural resources and polluting our world in the service of consumerism, we continue to use our technology and our advertising to produce and sell ever more goods. It appears, in fact, that we have created our economy so that unless our gross national product is constantly rising, we face a recession or a depression that punishes the workers who depend on our system for the necessities of life. Looking at things as they stand now, it seems that the unappealing choices are either to keep on wasting our resources and generating pollution or else face unemployment and starvation. Neither one satisfies the long-run need to survive.

Yet, the quality of our experiences as individuals and as a society is a function of our awareness. And awareness is a function of the mind's—and the social mind's—perception of reality. The kinds of experiences, joyful or painful, that we create in our daily lives, and the kinds of experiences that whole cultures create for themselves, are a matter of acting out of perceptions. These perceptions are recorded solely in congruence with existing mindsets. When we act out of sharply limited, say prejudicial, mindsets, we are likely to generate feedback that will reinforce our existing mindsets. Therefore, we are in danger of being caught up in an ever-tightening destructive spiral of our own making.

Common mindsets give populations, nations, and organizations "personality." Common fears among a people generate common subconscious defenses that influence the way nations react to problems and the actions of other nations. The conditions in which we live, as individuals or as people, generate common conscious "needs," values, and beliefs.

Leaders may either project their own vision of a powerful society on their people, or they can reflect the vision already held by the people. In either case they tend automatically to adjust their leadership to fit what the followers are programmed to perceive. An example of this social mind force was the way many Arabs throughout the world saw Saddam Hussein as a hero, even though he trampled the rights of a neighboring Arab state and lost a war. He was seen as a hero by many because he "stood up against" the evil Satan, the United States. His inhumane treatment of the Kuwaitis and the Kurds was overlooked by fellow Arabs who nurtured a deep-felt hatred of the United States and her western allies and were ready to rally around any powerful figure, however demented or demonic, who would war against the object of their hatred.

As you can imagine, we have a rather urgent need to upgrade the awareness of people everywhere, leaders and followers alike, and to convert more and more people from pro-gram-awareness, which is practically like running on automatic pilot, without real thinking or reflecting, to ego-mind-aware-ness, a much keener register. And those few leaders and decision makers who are already operating on some level of ego-mind-awareness need to be encouraged to continue the upward climb until they reach supra-consciousness, the pow-erful, transcendent state of awareness and commitment that radiates goodwill and wise counsel.

Only then will leaders be adequately open and able to re-ceive information on all the necessary channels, properly di-gest the data, and devise solutions that will be long-term, compassionate, and effective, instead of short-term, political, and palliative.

1. Kennedy, Paul, *Preparing for the Twenty-First Century*, NY: Random House, 1993, p. 52.
2. Wheatley, Margaret, *Leadership and the New Science*, SF: Berrett-Koehler, 1992, pp 104-105.
3. Humphrey, Vice President Hubert, speech, Bonn, Germany, 30 March 1967.
4. Kennedy, Paul, *Preparing...*, pp. 126-127.

Chapter Seven

SOCIAL MIND AND LEADERSHIP

All power is a trust;
we are accountable for its exercise.
From the people and for the people
all springs and all must exist.

—Benjamin Disraeli

As soon as we conceive of society as a living social organism, it becomes logically necessary to conceive of that social organism as possessing a mind—*a social mind.* Just as an individual's mind is separate from, but intimately connected to, a body, so does our society, or our social body, have a mind which is separate from but intimately connected to the social body. Like an individual's mind, the social mind is a storage place for mindsets. Some of these mindsets, or propensities, may, when put into action, lead to good or beneficial outcomes; others may lead to negative or damaging outcomes. When contradictory mindsets operate simultaneously, we have a social body that may be somewhat schizophrenic.

Social mind, on a global scale, consists of all the projected consciousness of billions of human beings, influenced by and filtered through the many cultures and through the interplays among those cultures. Behind all that multilayered consciousness are beliefs, concepts, values, attitudes, expectations, fears, habits, and wishes. These internalized systems of thinking and reacting are based on *perceptions of reality—not on objective reality.* These perceptions may be more or less in touch with reality depending on many variables—such as education levels, degree of freedom of speech and press, and the amount of contact with other cultures.

Let us note, however, that though we respond only to perceived reality, objective reality has real consequences for us. Many of us lived happily for generations eating fat foods and smoking cigarettes which we perceived as satisfying and harmless. New awareness of "reality" is leading to considerable change in social behavior. People lived for many years in a New England town contaminated by underground pollution that affected their drinking water without perceiving that they were poisoning themselves daily. To the town as a social organism, a glass of water was as harmless as it would have been in other parts of the country, and the town was perfectly satisfied with its water system. Only when their perceptions of reality were brought in line with the objective state of the polluted drinking water did they adjust their mindsets—and stop drinking the water and change their water system.

Objective reality refers to the way things really are in the physical world or in the social world. *Perceived reality* is the way the mind sees "what is" in the physical or social world. To understand this, one has to recognize that individuals do not experience the objective world *directly.* What people experience is their creation of what is "out there" as a function of what comes in through their senses, or what results from their mind's interpretation of what is coming in. Therefore, what a mind constructs may turn out to be vastly different from what actually *is*. For example, drivers approaching a curve on a highway may see the curve quite differently. For some it appears dangerous or threatening and they respond by cutting their speed by five or ten miles an hour; to others the curve appears engineered for normal speed and they zoom around it without slowing down whatsoever. The physical reality of that curve and its navigability may in fact lie at one extreme or the other, or somewhere in between.

The actual reality of our planet at the moment is that we are quite rapidly using up, altering, or destroying the natural state of our environment in service to acquisition needs that have been created in people through sophisticated marketing. The general interpretation of this situation in the social mind is that this level of consumption is appropriate and even of benefit. Nonetheless, the true physical and social reality may be that we are on the verge of destroying our life space.

To add one more example, many people perceive smoking cigarettes as an attractive and relatively innocuous pastime. The actual reality is that smoking is a fairly deadly endeavor—little more than incremental suicide. Still another illustration of the difference between objective and perceived reality can be understood from listening to smokers who want to quit but believe that doing so will be wrenchingly difficult. I myself was once a three-pack-a-day smoker, but reading the first cancer study issued by the government pointing out the dangers of smoking prompted me to quit smoking that night at midnight. The common perception of the reality of quitting conveyed to me the notion that the withdrawal symptoms would be all but unmanageable. The actual reality was that those symptoms did indeed provoke stress, tension, and nervousness, but I was able to handle them by simply telling myself that my body was merely reacting to deprivation of nicotine and that it would soon get over it. Within six weeks, not only did I no longer experience any urge to smoke, but I also had developed a great aversion to it. I did not buy into the marketeers' scenario that I would need hypnosis or chemicals to get me off cigarettes; I merely stopped cold. In other words I chose not to be ruled by the widely perceived difficulty of quitting this ravaging habit.

Another aspect of social mind that we need to consider is consciousness. Just as for an individual human, consciousness is necessary for the survival of the social body as a whole. At the simplest level, consciousness is merely awareness—being aware of and responsive to stimuli. A baby cries when its stomach signals that it is empty; it moves its bowels upon a signal from the colon; it reacts loudly and assertively to pain. In the adolescent human, hunger signals from the stomach propel the person toward the refrigerator. Such reactions are basically uncomplicated, automatic movements, almost instinctive rather than intuitive or rational actions.

To understand more clearly the importance and workings of the social mind, it will be helpful to compare it in some detail to operations in the individual mind. The mind of every individual may be seen as functioning at two significantly different levels. First and foremost, the mind operates in response to the needs and demands of the body, of the person of whom it is a part. The mind operates to avoid pain, to approach pleasure, to satisfy the needs and wants of the body, and, to a great extent, to meet the demands of ego. The mind operates at this level primarily in service of the immediate and personal needs and wishes of the individual. Let's call this "level one" mind functioning.

The second level at which the individual mind works is at that of the individual's relationship with the environment and with an abstraction we call "the future." In this function, rather than responding to the demands of direct stimuli, the mind looks ahead, anticipates the future and its consequences, and operates to position the person "now" for the best possible results in the perceived future. This is an abstract function of mind operating above and beyond the immediate processes of living. Many people do not operate extensively at this level, using their mind primarily for immediate functioning and satisfactions. Individuals who are more conscious and aware, however, are apt to use this higher level of mind consciousness in shaping their environment and future to suit anticipated needs and to avoid anticipated problems. Individuals who do not have the capacity for this kind of mind use, or who have not dedicated themselves to it, tend to live their lives as flotsam on the sea of chance.

These same two levels of functioning apply to the social mind. At the first and lower level of thinking, social mind is devoted to meeting the immediate cultural demands of society for safety, status, power, and comfort. At this level we see companies working hard to increase their own share of market, their profits, their dividends. We see politicians working doggedly for reelection and for passing legislation that will solve problems complained about by their constituencies. We find organizations working diligently to provide food and other care for starving populations around the world, and local cultures caught up in a push to clear their area of dangerous smog. We may also observe continual efforts to do away with beliefs and practices that foster racial discrimination. There are many such focuses of social mind at the immediate operating level. This is the level at which societies deal with their obvious problems and demands in order to sustain their overall well-being.

The social mind, however, is only beginning to be aware of the need for level two kind of thinking—projecting far into the future—and beginning to learn how to do it. The social organism is in a state similar to that of a teenager transitioning from childhood to adulthood, heavily focused upon acquiring the goods and resources for a happy, pleasant existence, and not giving much thought to creating the abstract future in a manner that will be safe, secure, and satisfying when the future arrives. Thinking at this level requires the organism to be aware of itself as a unity, and aware of the need to think of the well-being of that unity as necessarily dependent upon its interaction with the rest of the world. This is different from the level of mind operation that has to do with satisfying immediate—and proximate—needs.

Society is just barely beginning to develop a consciousness of itself as an organismic entity. Depending on how it decides to think and function, society will determine the quality of life and the duration of humanity in the future. The masses of individual minds, which make up the social mind, are just on the threshold of developing a consciousness that their survival is directly dependent, and increasingly so, on the survival of the social organism of which they are part.

For the social organism to engage effectively in the second level of thinking the underlying beliefs present in masses of millions of individual minds must give rise to that second-level consciousness in the social mind. This higher level of consciousness is needed in our social mind if society is to act as an entity to deal with problems that affect the possibility of our world's survival.

As humans mature, simple consciousness expands to the level of self-consciousness, that is, awareness of "self" as an important entity, something apart from, but in relation to, the rest of the world. As this self-consciousness develops, one can act not only automatically but also by intention, by power of will, by a deliberate decision taking of the mind. From non-self-consciousness, a person may act as a whole in automatic response to the urging of an organ, as when his stomach makes demands and provokes excessive and undisciplined eating, which leads to obesity. Acting from self-conscious will which says, "The appetite wants to eat, but I want my body to be thin, so I won't let my body eat," the same person is able to override the demands of the appetite to achieve a healthier condition for the entire body.

The same is true in the social mind. As society matures, it acquires consciousness of itself as an existing entity, with interrelationships among cultures, climates, and such human systems as commerce, communication, and transportation. It will, ideally, graduate from simple non-self-conscious automatic responses to external or internal stimuli, to intuitive and thought-out responses. It may come about, for example, that the United States becomes sufficiently conscious as a social body that it ignores the demands of its parts to the extent necessary to balance the national budget. As a self-aware social organism, we will give more concerted social thought to potential problems of overpopulation, overconsumption and destruction of irreplaceable resources, implicit new demands that will be imposed upon the educational processes, for developing our citizenry, and the simple and obvious problem of controlling the automatic increase of pollution that arises as a function of the activities of more and more consumers. Likewise, there may be more thinking about the extremely complicated problem of managing mankind in a manner that avoids the rapidly progressing destruction of other forms of life on the planet. At present we seem to be choking ourselves to death under the assumption that the expansion of human numbers justifies the destruction of the natural environment and the habitat of other living creatures as well as of the very air we ourselves must breathe.

As the social organism feels the need for the higher, and more intense, second-level thinking, it will give rise inevitably to an increasing demand for more, and more complicated, leadership. Part of the problem in developing this kind of leadership will be that it needs to focus upon solving abstract problems in ways that do not lead to any immediate gratification or reinforcement for those engaged in the action. In level-one thinking, solutions to problems do indeed lead to immediate gain, such as the comfort and convenience of having a new car. By way of contrast, our society's solving the population problem for the sake of people who may live two hundred years from now affords little concrete gratification to people living today.

Such dilemmas bring us to a key element in the process of developing self-consciousness—the leadership-element. This element is an important subset, or component, of the social mind. "Leaders" are themselves a part, but only a part, of the leadership-element. By their policies and actions they contribute mightily to its formation, but they are also shaped by other aspects of it. Those aspects include the methods by which leaders are trained and empowered, and in the context of culture, the means by which they maintain power, and public perceptions of, and control over a society's leaders.

Such control embraces general social, moral, and ethical standards, as well as public beliefs about, and public expectations for, leaders. Legal restraints and codes of conduct governing specific professions or sectors are other components of the leadership-element.

Leaders never operate in a cultural vacuum. They are limited by the permissions a culture grants and the limits it imposes on leaders. All of which is to say that they operate within the context of first a local social mind, and then a regional, a national, and finally a global social mind.

Thus leaders are a part of a larger entity called the leadership-element and the leadership-element needs to be seen as part of a still vaster phenomenon called the social mind.

The ramifications of the social mind upon our lives are many and complex. The United States believes in free enterprise; Russia formerly put its faith in state planning and control—and may one day decide to do so again. (The reason, in fact, that capitalism has not yet taken hold well in parts of the former Soviet Union is that people there do not have the mindsets for it. They have had trouble understanding and accepting it, and many have already decided that they really don't want to acquire capitalistic, or democratic, mindsets at all.) Homosexuals believe that sexual behavior between consenting adults is a private matter; some other members of society believe that legitimizing such behavior constitutes a public evil. Free enterprise members in growing sectors of the economy favor freedom of trade and non-interference by government; members of sectors severely undercut by foreign competition, on the other hand, want trade barriers, tariffs, and government subsidies. Certain groups, from the IRA to radical Palestinian and Jewish groups to anarchists, believe that terrorism is a valid and legitimate instrument of social struggle; most people hold that terrorism is not only reprehensible but also criminal. Ecologists believe that production, profits, and economic expansion should be curtailed to protect the environment. Others believe they have a right to unbridled expansion of their particular industry, and let the ecological consequences be damned.

Still more examples of conflicting values and operations in our social mind would include proponents versus opponents of abortion rights, those pushing for stiffer and longer sentences for people convicted of violent crimes versus those campaigning for prison reform and for spending more money on changing the environment and ghetto neighborhoods, educators trying to break down barriers in the school and foster more integration versus students asserting their rights to self-segregate and promote subgroups (i.e., ethnic) values. The list, indeed, is long.

The point of all these examples is that the social mind, just like mine or yours, has many beliefs and programs, and many of them contradict each other. *This important reality of the social mind needs to be appreciated by all who lead.*

The social mind contains many negatives. For example, a large number of people appear determined to keep on smoking, even though it is known that smoking causes cancer and that cancer kills. Moreover, people continue to stress themselves into breakdowns and heart attacks while chasing the hope of materialist nirvana, despite being quite bored and unhappy with many elements of the chase—long commutes and office hours, high-tension working conditions, etc. The social mind consists of and acts out of the same kind of contradictions as commonly found in the individual mind—probably to a greater degree.

To the extent that such differences of mindsets and beliefs exist in the social mind, to that extent will it remain difficult for the social organism to arrive at a focused and thought-out program of second-level thinking for the management and evolution of the social body.

HIGHER FUNCTIONS OF SOCIAL MIND

Notwithstanding these internal conflicts, the social mind is the controlling, directing, integrating, and energizing force within the social body. Without a mind, the social body can no more direct itself than can any other body. However, because of a relatively low level of congruence and harmony in the social mind as it is constituted today, we have experienced considerable malaise and drift in late twentieth-century society. One result is that it seems impossible for the social organism of the planet to make up its mind that wars are foolish, pointless, and serve no useful end. Despite the pain and suffering they cause, the world continues to engender wars.

One part of the social mind operates as an automatic central switchboard. This part, which corresponds to level-one thinking, routinely responds to signals from within the body and routes responses so as to keep normal everyday operations in order. Thus just as a part of the human being's peripheral nervous system increases blood supply to the stomach when the body needs energy for digestion, so does a corporation's purchasing department respond automatically to acquire more raw materials when sales generate additional orders.

Above this is a higher order of mind that is aware of the needs and purposes of the organism as a whole. This is level-two thinking for the social body. This level directs attention in interactions with the environment and moves the entire body in response to perceived opportunities or threats. It automatically overrides—or tries to—lower-level demands that interfere with or contradict the social body's need. The parched throat of a man crossing a desert will cry out for water. But the mind may reject that demand because it knows it must conserve water in order to survive on the morrow. Corporate top management may similarly override the urgent request of one of its divisions for a bigger budget because it is trying to use its resources to improve the position of the entire company in the marketplace. A still higher aspect of social mind is a part that is aware of its awareness. In the individual human mind this consciousness is experienced as the self, the ego, the will power, the conscious "I."

As social consciousness rises, the leadership learns to act self-consciously through deliberate will power to override automatic habitual responses that deal only with the narrow self-interest of one part of the social body. The Gulf War illustrates this. Now leaders are acting in concert to negotiate new ways to cope with pressing social needs. John Kenneth Galbraith refers to this willingness as an essential part of the nature of true leaders: "All of the great leaders," he writes, "have had one characteristic in common: it (is) the willingness to confront unequivocally the major anxiety of their people in their time."[1] This process is imperative if, for example, the U.S. government is ever to gain control of its budget deficit. It is imperative if the nations of the world are to protect the ozone layer from destruction by industrial by-products. It is imperative, in fact, if we as a global society are to avert impending catastrophe in any number of sectors, such as, to take one more example, a drastic increase in the tendency in parts of the social organism to engage in terrorism and other forms of social body destruction out of level-one thinking directed to *their* part of the body.

Recently we have had some clear signals that the leader-ship-element is becoming properly self-conscious. Such signs were evident in the allied coalition's handling of the Persian Gulf Crisis. Iraq, under the dictatorial leadership of Saddam Hussein, moved to satisfy its—or his—needs by invading and occupying neighboring Kuwait. From the viewpoint of Iraq as a part of the global whole, this was a gainful move. Implicit in the move, however, were serious threats to the stability and well-being of society at large.

Not only did the Iraqi invasion of Kuwait signal an attempt by Saddam Hussein to gain control of the Middle Eastern oil resources, upon which much of the world depends for fuel, it also jolted nations near and far into the realization of Saddam's progress in developing immense military power for aggressive purposes. If such mindsets are allowed to run rampant, the peace and stability many peoples hope for will be forever at risk. Just as the human body has trouble surviving when one part becomes cancerous, so does the social body find that its survival is challenged if certain institutions or governments pillage and overrun other parts of the global society. Although empire building has a long history dating back even beyond Alexander the Great, only in the twentieth century has the world seen the potential for planetary devastation through nuclear weapons and germ warfare. The times in which we have been living are, indeed, quite perilous.

An important feature of the Persian Gulf episode was the surprisingly clear emergence of a supra-leadership approach. One sign of social mind control in the overview I have been depicting was the restraint and long delay in response to Iraq's aggression. Leaders from all over the world engaged in discussion and argument as to the proper response for the world to make. The United States and Saudi Arabia worked together to build an amazing coalition of Arab and western nations to assert, as one, that aggression such as Saddam's gambit in Kuwait was not acceptable. The United Nations, a supra-leadership organization in its very essence and character, provided the overall forum for debate for the resolution to check Saddam's ploy by military force. Israel, though hit by Iraqi missiles aimed at its population centers, held back its formidable retaliatory potential in order to avoid disrupting the leader-element coalition that was seeking to halt and to outlaw aggression.

The existence and impact of the United Nations itself speaks rather eloquently to a recognized need in our world for a supra-national approach to global issues.

After the devastation of World War II, certainly with a view to containing fascistic aggression in the future, the community of nations—though it barely understood itself as a "community" at the time—came together to institute the United Nations. The UN and its numerous satellite agencies, such as the World Health Organization and the Food and Agricultural Organization, gave us the first large-scale working example of a supra-national vision. Since the founding of the UN in 1947, a number of other bodies have come into being and currently provide us with still other working examples of supra-nationalism and supra-leadership. Among these we now count such institutions as the World Bank, the World Council of Churches, the Interpol Network of Police Cooperation, and the World Wildlife Federation. There are many, many more.

On a national scale, the founding fathers of the United States of America were extraordinarily farsighted in conceiving a system that provided for overall federal control of certain institutions, while vesting powerful, though limited, autonomy in the governments of the individual states. Such decentralization was theretofore unknown in the history of world governments. This notion, which later came to be known as the "principle of subsidiarity," was strongly lauded and endorsed by Pope John XXIII in his encyclical "Pacem in Terris" on ways to promote global well-being and peace. The brilliant conceptualizing of levels of government to respond to needs that were national, regional, or local, and the actual putting into practice of the principle of subsidiarity probably go far toward explaining the general economic and political success of the United States on the world scene.

In all periods of human history, in all social and civil contexts, there has always been a social mind and there has always been a leadership-element. The difference now is that we have evolved rapidly in the twentieth century into a global society that is far more populous, interdependent, and technologically sophisticated than was ever true in the past. That is why today's world leadership-element has become so critical for keeping ecological, social, economic, and political systems in productive synergy.

Historically, most leadership has been a response to the needs of social units acting very much in their own self-interest. This "part-oriented" mindset still predominates, even though global society has become increasingly holistic and interrelated. Despite tremendous efforts on the part of scientists and government officials to educate the community about pollution, we still have to monitor dumping and emissions carefully. Otherwise certain industrial components of society will seize the cheapest and "most efficient" means of waste disposal and simply dump effluent into streams, lakes, rivers, or the ocean. Enough of such dumping will poison or destroy marine life and "kill" a particular body of water.

SUPRA-CONSCIOUS LEADERSHIP

THE DRAINING EFFECT OF LEADERSHIP-LAG

Even though we are making progress toward achieving more social body self-consciousness among our leaders, currently their mindsets still tend to restrict planning to immediate goals, to followers' needs and responses, and to actions required for short-term success. Because of this, business leaders make decisions that engender profits for their firms and secure their personal power, but nonetheless undermine the free-enterprise system that they claim to support. Common examples are current trends toward gigantic cartels created to control whole industries and markets, squeezing out smaller competitors, price fixing, bid rigging, and many other forms of illegal or unethical corporate behavior. On the other side of the ledger, unions may push for unreasonable wage concessions that may play into the hands of foreign competitors and drive a local company to bankruptcy.

All of these examples indicate a continuing allegiance to old mindsets that are no longer suited—if they ever were—to a realistic understanding of what society needs for its own survival. "A state without the means of some change," we need to remind ourselves that Edmond Burke cautioned us, "is without the means of its own conservation."[2]

Such dangerous reliance upon outdated mindsets in the face of pressing socioeconomic realities of global interdependency constitutes a "leadership-lag." By this I mean simply that we are trying to solve today's problems with yesterday's understandings. It won't work. It seems, however, that until failures stemming from the use of old mindsets force both leaders and followers off "automatic pilot," the inertia attached to the old patterns will inhibit necessary change. How long such obtuseness will prevail probably will depend upon the gravity of our failures and the rigidity of attachments to worn-out mindsets.

The leadership-lag of which I am speaking is the source of a great deal of confusion, disruption, conflict, and frustration in our rapidly evolving society.

One thing ought to be clear: it is not enough simply to lead one's own organization as if in a social vacuum. All leaders are responsible, or should be, for becoming aware of the larger repercussions of their leadership—repercussions upon their companies, their industries, their communities, their regions—and their planet. If they do not choose to accept such responsibility freely, the choice will be forced upon us by upheavals of nature and by the collapse of human systems now held in place by very fragile underpinnings.

---

1. Galbraith, John Kenneth, *The Age of Uncertainty,* 1974. Boston: Houghton Mifflin, 1977.
2. Burke, Edmund, "Reflections on the Revolution in France," 1790.

Chapter Eight

NEEDED: SUPRA-CONSCIOUS LEADERS

These are hard times
in which a genius would wish to live.
Great necessities call forth great leaders.
— Abigail Adams
in a letter to Thomas Jefferson

Though most people are not aware of it, all leaders, from the highest to the lowest—be they foremen or heads of state— are always responsible for two goals in their domains. The first is to assure the successful accomplishing of whatever tasks are necessary for producing a quality product or service. I call this "task-leadership." The second goal is to protect and promote—or "support," if you like—*the overall social good (what some of the early framers of the Constitution referred to as "the common wealth").* This I have chosen to label "supra-leadership."

Supra-Leadership

The term supra-leadership refers to that quality of leadership that produces effects that are beyond (overarching or "supra") the intended result in the leader's immediate realm of operations. Supra-leadership is that which, *either by intention or as a by-product of task-leadership*, has a positive or negative effect on the larger organization, the community, or the wider society in which a leader and his or her followers are carrying out their production tasks.

The fact that so many leaders overlook the supra-leadership effects of their decisions and actions shows how much they underestimate the importance to the broader society of what they do at work every day. They are too nearsighted; they see their role exclusively as keeping the day's operations on track. Often, they don't even really see themselves as leaders, but as managers or supervisors, riding herd on quality control and warehousing, or making sure that all the eighteen-wheelers are rolling toward their destinations, or nailing down the final numbers on an audit.

What they may not see, however, are the unintended negative supra-leadership effects of their decisions and actions. A company may produce profits for stockholders and please its customers with products but the firm's manufacturing process may provoke acid rain that destroys forests. It is good for chemical companies that so many farmers around the world rely upon pesticides to protect their crops; however, we all suffer from the inevitable supra-effect of poison accumulating in the food chain.

Even those who do see the larger effects of what they do are likely to place too much value on day-to-day outcomes as compared to possible impacts on the greater good. That does not mean their daily outcomes are not important. Their task-leadership is essential to society. Obviously, task-leadership needs to get done, and done well, otherwise governments, organizations, and companies cannot chart their way through the shoals of turbulent times and merciless competition. If the millions of task leaders do not get their work done, and do it well, there will be no goods for us to buy, and no jobs for us to have.

In past times, a focus on task-leadership sufficed for society. If every leader simply "minded the store," the larger picture got worked out by politicians, activists, and the give-and-take among special interest groups and by citizens reacting to what they experienced, or to what was reported in the media. Now, to survive as a global society in perilous synergy, we have an absolute need to become supra-conscious in our leadership. That is to say, among other things, we need social recognition that every leader's importance goes beyond the specific task for which he or she is responsible. To some degree, large or small, the ripple effects of a leader's actions trigger repercussions not only for the larger organization in which the leader works, but also for the community, the region, the nation, and ultimately the planet. A head of government fostering industrial growth may do so in a manner that either leaves business free to generate acid rains and destroy the forests, or in a way that protects and enhances the environment. A foreman may get his unit's work out on time either in a manner that dehumanizes his workers by turning them into cogs in a production line, or in a way that promotes the workers' sense of responsible involvement in their company's success. The CEO of a textile mill may build a thriving company while contaminating the air and local waterways, or seek to harmonize production with respect for the vital elements upon which the community depends for its quality of life. A school superintendent may run a curriculum in which teaching fosters love of learning, or in which it stifles motivation to study and learn.

Along with bringing us many blessings, science has also provided us with the power to destroy our world. It has, in fact, made doing so a rather simple affair. One leader with the insanity of a Hitler can push a button and start a chain reaction of nuclear explosions, and reactions from other nations, that could devastate the planet, wiping out millions of human lives. One error in a bacterial warfare laboratory might release into the atmosphere a lethal disease-bearing agent, with similar kill-power. Technical decisions business leaders make now have the potential to pollute huge regions or turn the earth into a place too hot to live in.

Conditions of interdependency are now such that even less-lethal "errors" can wreak chaos. Within a single business unit the head of manufacturing can increase production in a manner that conflicts with the findings from the market research department. An industry's successful lobbying for higher tariffs can make it unnecessary for that industry to meet efficient competition from abroad, thereby undermining its long-term effectiveness in the world market. "Small" local armed conflicts can quickly spread and engulf neighboring states—or even states farther away.

In the past fifty years especially, the rate of social change and growth has become explosive. The consequences of this largely unplanned hyper-growth for the leadership-element are significant. Currently, the challenge and complexity of leadership problems exceed our ability to deal with them effectively. Society is world encompassing, highly interrelated and interdependent—a sensitive drumskin that reverberates to even the slightest tap. Things have changed much faster than human mindsets can adapt by the slow and undirected process of natural evolution.

Leaders struggle to catch up with growing demands for better and more powerful leadership. They do so mostly, however, by calling upon leadership mindsets shaped by non-self-conscious trial-and-error evolution of the past. We can no longer afford such a bumbling approach. It results in the "leadership-lag" that has us relying upon leadership models that fit the past but do not suit the present. Trial-and-error evolution is an effective approach if the errors are not fatal and the changes are slow paced enough for people to be able to adapt to them. Our world has developed to such a high state of power and interdependency, however, that errors that previously might have remained without significant impact for years now have instantaneous negative consequences on part or all of humanity. They even have potential to destroy the world, a possibility we did not have to worry about in the past.

It may be important to note that supra- or overarching effects are not restricted to leadership. They occur in almost all social interactions—in families, in schools, in hospitals, and in many non-work situations. In short, in our highly interconnected world, *most* actions of any significance have ripple effects on others. Some of those effects are minimal and virtually unobservable, while others have immense impact on the community, the ecosphere, and social systems. Commuting to work by car seems efficient for people who are thus able to live in a bucolic suburb yet earn their living downtown. However, with so many people having the same idea about getting to work, we have thousands of cars pumping carbon monoxide into the air over our metropolitan areas. This is a negative supra-effect of the commuting syndrome. Even more subtly, it may satisfy some adults to express their frustrations out loud when things go awry on the homefront. However, over time, the supra-effect of such venting may be to teach their children to refrain from expressing themselves for fear of provoking an authority figure's anger. Such suppression can engender negative programs that will greatly restrict personality growth. If you give a child too much free-dom, you can end up with an adult who does not know how to conform enough to get along in society. On the other hand, if you constrain children too much, they may grow up without the assertiveness needed to cope in a competitive society.

I should also mention here that what I call supra-leader-ship has rarely been clearly defined or published with much resonance up to now. Supra-leadership effects are often very subtle, are nonimmediate, and may impact parts of the world that are outside the range of our mental and physical vision. It is difficult to pay attention to something that is hard to see or to define. That does not make it any less dangerous to ignore. Even though somewhat abstract and sometimes hard to get across, the concept of supra-leadership absolutely needs to be deeply understood by trailblazers leading us into new cultural frontiers.

Therefore, while it is not possible to do away entirely with trial-and-error processes and effects, it behooves us to become considerably more self-conscious in the ways we develop and carry out the leadership-element role. We need to develop ways to ensure that all leaders are aware of and responsible for supra-leadership effects as well as for task-leadership out-comes, and that they meet those responsibilities under guid-ance of a clear and formal code of leader ethics. (And in the capstone chapter of this book, I shall set forth my own draft of such a code, a draft which I hope will provide the basis for wide-ranging debate and the hammering out of tenets with broad international support.) We need much more social attention to the process of selecting and training leaders who hold peoples' lives in their hands by virtue of their role. Lead-ership, after all, is a social resource of the greatest significance to our well-being—and our survival. It is in everybody's interest to have leaders adopt new guiding role models that better fit their decision-making processes to current global conditions.

Likewise, *followers* need new concepts of what they are willing to accept from their leaders. *After all, followers decide what leadership is; in other words, "true" leadership is nothing more nor less than that which followers agree to respect and comply with.* This means that leaders and followers alike have to make some adjustments in our understanding of what leadership is and how, ideally, it should operate.

We need to change our present social concept of leaders' roles. The present concept—occasionally explicit, often implicit and unconscious—shapes leadership mainly within the understanding of direct leader roles and leader tasks. We need training and concepts that include much more consideration of larger social responsibility, or supra-leadership. At present, in too many cases, the main directing force is the self-serving interest of the leader. This is what at all costs must change if we hope to survive as a healthy, vibrant society.

A Journey Toward Change

In the process of reading this book, ideally, you are journeying toward a change in your mindsets. This is a critical adventure, because we are all—leaders and followers alike—limited by whatever mindsets we have stored in our minds. To the extent those mindsets have been producing effective outcomes for us, we let them run us automatically. That means we keep on doing what we have always done, even though it may no longer be the best approach. Until things get so bad that they fall apart, we stay on our old path—and probably blame the negatives that occur on someone else. If we want to deal with situations that call for change before things fall apart, we must "go off automatic" and deliberately install within ourselves some new mindsets.

Under trial-and-error evolution, a leader's mindsets develop in reaction to two things: 1) their experience with life and leadership problems on the firing line, and 2) their response to leadership beliefs and attitudes passed on by earlier generations.

Most leaders learned their role in relatively compartmentalized social cells in which problems tended to be direct and immediate. A foreman who had to get the work cranked out had little awareness that as things changed his leadership was eroding worker motivation and hence was bad for the long term. A city manager who had a surplus of garbage on hand decided the city's trucks would dump it in the country. He was not aware of the need for measures to protect underground streams that carried the pollution into farmers' fields. All he knew was that his city was rid of the garbage. Local success, pure and simple. The garbage was out of sight and hence out of mind. If it caused problems elsewhere, then somebody else would deal with it there.

The social product of this historical experience has been a generalized leader mindset to think and react in terms of specific, concrete, and short-term problems and goals. Too little thought has gone into the consideration of the effects of a solution beyond the immediate impact on profit and loss statements or the outcome of the next election. Too many political actions are based on a need to "support the party," rather than on what is good for the country. Even within the structure of one company, if there is a need to consider potential benefits to another unit or department, thinking is frequently couched in "us" and "them" terms, or "win or lose," or, at best, "let's cooperate to the extent that we get what we want."

Extrapolating from the same principle on the international scale, the United States and the Soviet Union, until quite recently, used their veto power in the United Nations to promote narrow nationalistic interests rather than to support the greater good of the planet. And certain nations still use this shortsighted approach by continuing to kill whales even though the shrinking whale population is approaching the endangered species line.

One of the most pervasive mistakes being made by American business leaders has been failing to pay enough attention to serving the greater good through management-employee relations. Serving the greater good of employees should be a key objective of supra-conscious business leadership. Here the greater good means not only the workers' economic well-being, but also their sense of worth and their capacity for citizenship and fully human living. Serving this greater good will make workers a more integral part of successful operations. Such workers will exhibit increased motivation, creativity, and responsibility and will find more satisfaction and pleasure in their work. As leaders experiment more with expanding worker participation, we shall find that the American work force represents a vast reservoir of social contribution and creativity just waiting to be tapped.

Serving the greater good is a key component of supra-conscious leadership. Often, when an American company's profitability slips toward the red, and downsizing is seized upon as a solution, the executives seem to be more chagrined over the loss of stockholder earnings than over the destruction of work spaces upon which employees rely for their economic well-being. In light of past management practices, downsizing may actually be necessary at times. However, the work spaces that leaders supervise and control are also the personal life spaces of the people who work for them. Generally, people have few alternatives to submitting to someone else's leadership in order to make a living.

As they struggle with fairness issues, leaders will constantly find themselves up against conflicts between greater goods and greater negatives. Serving one greater good, such as boosting workers' pay, results in a new challenge for profitability as a company. These conflicts are inevitable in the process of running a complex society, and particularly in running a democratic world where the primary goal is to achieve and respect a balance between the rights and demands of various elements—capitalists seeking a return on their money, salaried workers seeking a return on their talent and investment of time and energy, and hourly workers seeking higher wages and better benefits.

Conflicts among various constituencies are inherent in leading and managing society and its multiple units. Such conflicts cannot be avoided. What is good for one group is not necessarily good for another, and quite often it will even contradict their good. Millions of people would be healthier if we stopped producing cigarettes and other smoking materials. Doing so, however, would truncate a financial base that currently supports a large portion of the population. Workers would gain if they received the lion's share of companies' profits. Giving it to them, however, could reduce the earnings benefits to stockholders, thereby reducing their investments, and it could raise prices to the public thereby reducing sales, and perhaps driving the organization out of business.

Leaders too often pay too little attention to how their leadership affects the satisfactions, ego needs, morale, motivations, and home lives of their subordinates. Constant treatment of employees—or citizens—as human cogs, as something bought and paid for, as workers who are simply there to "do as they are told," as nonparticipants in the creative or problem-solving aspects of the organization, results in a passive, unmotivated, even disaffected work force.

The industrial revolution created industries that use organized, mechanized, and highly structured production processes to produce valuable products for society and profits for shareholders. This has resulted in a greatly increased standard of living. Production processes, however, have become highly automated, and have tended to reduce employees to the role of human cogs in carefully structured assembly lines that are mass productive. People are fit into closely defined, narrowly conceived roles to perform repetitive functions that call for almost no responsibility for outcome, creative thinking, decision making, or in many cases any understanding of the product being turned out. The system, nevertheless, has been efficient and profitable.

Though providing effective task-leadership for producing goods for society and profits for shareholders, the great majority of leaders perform poorly in the realm of supra-leadership with respect to followers. They challenge employees to very little growth, ego involvement, or responsibility for taking an active part in the company's role of supporting society. Employees are conscious of working only to "do my job"— not for any sense of higher social purpose. Such a narrow work ethic is deadening. Potential challenge and stimulation in the work environment are cut off at the root. Morale is left to sag.

Consider a particular production department foreman in the above industrial system who is responsible and hard working. The man is a careful planner who gets the work out on time and produces high quality products because he is a clear, direct supervisor who asks for what he wants and then follows up to be sure that he gets it. He is ethical and courteous in dealing with his people, and he believes they are a vital resource of the organization. However, the foreman seldom asks for his people's opinions or asks them to help solve problems of operations or of the working environment.

Except for his commitment to respect and courtesy, this foreman is largely unaware of his supra-leadership role. Over the years his approach teaches his workers to act "as a pair of hands" or as human equipment. They learn not to be responsible for anything beyond their assigned task. They learn that they have nothing other than labor to contribute, that it is not important that what they know be heard, and that management expects no input or participation from them beyond doing what they are told to do. So, while the foreman's task-leadership is effective because it gets the job done, his supra-leadership impact is negative. When a worker leaves the organization and moves to a new job somewhere else, he or she carries along that same attitude of nonresponsible passivity.

Such supra-leadership effects are destructive to the greater good of companies, the community, and society. As should be evident to everyone, the health of all three social units depends on the physical, emotional, and mental health of members—who are, after all, not just "workers," but also consumers, citizens, neighbors, and mothers and fathers.

A still prevalent business rationalization for inattention to human needs of employees, or community needs of citizens, is the laissez faire attitude that, "My job is to do the best I can to 'win' for my company by making a profit. If I do that, it means the competitive forces of the marketplace are working automatically to balance things out for the greater good."

This attitude was nicely capsuled in the celebrated epithet of Daddy Warbucks, the tycoon figure in Al Capp's Orphan Annie cartoon strip (1940s through '60s): "What's good for Daddy Warbucks is good for America."

That may have been true in the underdeveloped culture that gave birth to free market industrialization, but it is not effective in our highly integrated and overconsuming society. The "laissez faire" argument often is merely support for a leader mindset of nonresponsibility for anything but his or her own immediate domain, and let the rest of the (interdependent) world take care of itself. This position, usually adopted unconsciously, is becoming more untenable every day.

Changing our mindsets so that we think, reflect, and react differently as leaders and followers from the ways of the past is a process that each of us must consciously decide to engage in if we are going to keep our mindsets in sync with the rapidly changing world. The process is neither simple nor painless, but it will be rewarding—for ourselves and for the lives of those who depend on our policies and actions.

To get ahead of the slow pace of trial-and-error mindset change, we must actively choose to become aware of what has been happening to our society, of how we have been performing in our own roles, and of how we might change that performance to reflect a supra-conscious perspective and commitment. And we must seek to enlist others in the struggle.

If you lead for the good of everyone you must learn to see your role as much more important and much broader than mere "task-leadership" or "minding the store." The ways you lead—and the leadership you reinforce when you accept it as a follower—have repercussions outside your unit, outside even your own company; your leadership affects your employees' personal lives, their families, and the tenor of the wider community. When anyone takes on responsibility as a leader at any level—in the office, in school, at church, in community-service bodies such as the Boy Scouts, or the hospital's volunteers corps—that person inevitably also shoulders some responsibility for the shaping and well-being of society.

LEADERSHIP DETERMINES QUALITY OF LIFE

There is an urgent need for us as individuals *and as an organized society* to take the conscious, responsible steps I have outlined above to manage our leadership-element as a crucial force that determines the quality of our lives. Having good leadership is absolutely essential to keeping on with the game we call civilization. Being responsible for supra-leadership effects does not mean, of course, that it is good leadership to do so to the point where the organization you may be leading is damaged. Movement down the path toward a more positive society is a process of constant yin/yang variation around a point of best balance between the immediate good and the greater good. The value of creativity can be enjoyed only at the cost of change, and sometimes that change may result in an immediate cost. It takes careful leadership to determine if the greater good is worth the immediate cost.

One function of proper supra-leadership is to spot problems on the horizon that require action today in order to head off impending chaos. Consider, for example, the problem of overpopulation. Our globe can accommodate only a finite amount of humanity. We are already reaching the level where the mass of humanity is beginning to destroy the very environment needed to support it. Nevertheless, there is scant task-leadership and even less supra-leadership oriented toward determining and achieving a sustainable world population. There seems to be an underlying social assumption that the population will regulate itself. That may well be so, but, if

Malthus' theories are on target, the evolutionary methods that will provide such regulation are likely to be quite painful.

Our great school system for providing universal education works hard to educate our children, and to create and to measure the effectiveness of teaching. A universal system of grading performance on a scale ranging from A to F guides teachers, gives administrators the means for evaluating teachers, informs parents how their children are doing, and, most importantly, tells students themselves how they are doing. Motivational pressure and the sense of achievement for students tends to be based on the distribution of grades along a curve. Those whose performance is graded as above the mean —A and B—are rewarded with the right to feel proud and effective. Those whose performance is graded at or below the mean—D and F—get to feel ashamed or inadequate. And both groups learn that, if they want to receive good grades, they must dedicate themselves to learning whatever it is that the system has determined constitutes a "good education."

Whatever the benefits of this system—and there are many— it appears to produce some real and important *negative* supra-leadership effects. Because about half of our pupils are on the bottom of the curve, our system teaches them to feel incompetent as a function of their learning experience in school. The other half get to feel superior. It may be argued that learning either of these attitudes is a negative supra-leadership outcome for our citizens. The system also tells people that the aim of education is to be sure that they "fit the mold," rather than that they learn who they are and how to make the best of such talents and energies as they naturally possess. Those on the lower end of the scholastic ability range learn that education is difficult and painful to the ego; therefore, they practice avoidance of learning and thereby ensure that they will minimize their contribution to the sane development of society. How much better might the world be if the leaders of the school system paid less attention to the "normal curve" and instead ran the system on the assumption *that all humans are capable of being happy, loving, and productive and that the highest goal of the educational system is to help each individual be all he or she can be.* That would be a marvelous example of positive supra-leadership.

As followers too (as virtually all of us are followers at least in relation to those who lead our country politically) we need to pay more attention to, and exert more control over, the quality of leadership we support. After all, it is followers who make the leaders, because until someone follows, you don't have a leader. So often we do not realize, or else we forget, that leaders have no power at all until someone decides to give it to them. At a fundamental level, we create our leaders because we need them to help us meet our needs. Few followers, however, act as if they have caught on to this truth. Most followers tend to greatly underestimate their power.

What we need is a more unified, self-conscious social body —without so much pulling apart of things by conflicting special interests heedless of the common good. And this body, ideally a professional body, must have supra-leadership from supra-leaders who are supported by intelligent, aware followers.

Some will say that all this sounds utopian, chimeric. My reply is, maybe so, but the hour is late and the alternatives— chaos and social breakdown—are not pretty. We need to build into the minds of our citizens, and especially those who lead, a *moral-ethical compass* that keeps them on a path that leads not only to their immediate goals, but also to the greater good for all. *This will not happen until we—as a society—focus our attention on making it happen.*

Chapter Nine

THE TRUE ENEMY: RESISTANCE TO AWARENESS

Man is made by his beliefs.
As he believes, so he is.

—Bhagavad-Gita

Leaders who act primarily according to their automatic programming usually force solutions that fit their mindsets rather than shape solutions that fit the demands of the problem. This tendency is the basic source of leadership-lag. In a culture of dynamic and constant change, such as we are now experiencing, reliance upon such automated reaction systems curtails the potential for creative and adaptive reactions.

John W. Gardner reminds us: "A society whose maturing consists simply of acquiring more firmly established ways of doing things is headed for the graveyard—even if it learns to do these things with greater and greater skill. In the ever-renewing society, what matures is a system or framework within which continuous innovation, renewal and rebirth can occur." [1]

In daily processes of living, the ability to use automated programs is a convenience and an asset. It allows us to devote our energies to living an enjoyable life rather than to deciding how to react to each and every stimulus. However, society, and particularly society's leaders, need to become aware of the limiting effects of solutions produced by automated, stuck-in-the-past, decision-making processes. Leaders who lead from automated programs have little ability to take us through the innovations we must make in order to keep up with rapidly changing conditions.

If we stop long enough to become aware of the problems caused by mind automation, we must then move into the inevitably painful processes of examining our mindsets, evaluating their fit to current situations, and charting courses of realistic change. It should be noted that the first stage of realistic change will be to focus on the mindsets in use, not the applications that new mindsets might make in a situation. In other words, developing new behaviors must be accomplished, fundamentally, through self-awareness and self-evaluation.

If leaders commit themselves deliberately to keeping minds programmed in ways appropriate to arising conditions, they will be able to lead a sane evolution of civilization into the next century. Further, people who move toward healthy mindset changes will force leaders into new patterns that work.

Therefore, one of the primary tasks that leaders must recognize and begin to address is leading the population, their followers, to reprogram their minds as required: leadership in a rapidly changing world must, of necessity, take the form of reeducation. Of course, getting things done ("task-leadership") must continue simultaneously.

The problems posed by a crippling federal deficit offer an example of the need for reeducation. At present, most elected officials seem to manipulate budgets according to current demands of the public. As a result, the public debt continues to increase. If leaders helped voters understand why and how to change their demands, they would truly be serving the public and might continue to hold office even after reducing the panoply of government services that cause the deficit.

Leaders are constantly faced with the challenge of turning intentions into actions. In order to succeed, they cannot stop after merely setting forth their objectives, nor after making sure their words have been properly understood by followers. In fact, they cannot even start with issuing commands. As we move to the higher levels of leadership our increasingly complex society is calling for, leaders will need to consciously lead and manage the process and expression of consciousness by their followers. The first step is to discern the existing awarenesses of the followers they seek to influence.

Followers react to the world in terms of the way they see it —in terms, that is, of their awareness of it. That awareness is shaped by their mindsets as well as by what exists "out there" in the world. A leader who seeks to get a response from a follower by offering or creating a stimulus "out there" that he values as positive will fail to get the desired response if he or she is unaware that in the follower's mind that stimulus is perceived as unpleasant. For example, if I think you like me I will expect a response from you quite unlike that which I will get if the fact of the matter is that you don't like me. As a leader, if I were aware that you didn't like me, I could more objectively select an approach that might get a less negative response. If I am leading followers in a situation on the assumption that they see it as a supportive and positive environment, whereas in fact they see it as threatening and hostile, my leadership will be ineffective. If, on the other hand, I am aware of my followers' view of the situation as hostile and threatening, I can generate communication that will temper the effects of their negative view.

Since the mind is the instrument that both receives and transmits all leadership and all followership perceptions and actions, any effort to develop effective patterns of leading or following must, consequently, begin with an appreciation of the relationships among persona, mind, and mindsets. *Since people are doing what they are doing according to the fit of their mindsets, if you want them to do something different, you must persuade them to change their mindsets to fit the new desired behavior.*

To be a truly skillful leader, therefore, requires two things. First, the leader must recognize and manage mindsets as needed to produce leadership in the form called for by each situation, rather than simply apply an automated approach that constitutes his or her "leadership style." Second, the leader must recognize that followers can only give a response that fits the programs they have in place, and that if such a response does not satisfy the demands of the leadership problem, *then the leader's basic task becomes one of influencing those he leads to change their mindsets as needed to get the desired outcome.*

TACTICS OF LEADERS

Here are the tactics leaders typically employ:

-*teaching*

-*reasoning*

-*feedback*

-*rewards*

-*force*

Even though they were generally not doing so on the basis of awareness of the nature of their task, leaders have always made use of *all* the above approaches—singly or in combinations—to get people to do what leaders wanted. Rather than go methodically through the steps of teaching, reasoning, and feedback, however, the traditional leader has tended to start with the *end* of the sequence—threats, or *force*. It does not have to be overt, bald-faced power; it may be simply that the leader owns the company or has the power to fire people. In fact, the traditional leader has most often *reversed* the sequence, starting with force in its varied forms and working back to teaching. Leaders, like everyone else, typically prefer what they perceive as the easiest approach available. Obviously, if you have power, or authority, the easiest form of leadership is to provide negative incentives for your followers: "Get this right or you'll be fired." "Meet your sales quota or else you'll lose out on your bonus." And, more subtly, bosses often manage to communicate something that goes like, "Be sure you please me personally as well as accomplish all your assigned tasks, or you'll probably be passed over for promotion."

Next comes *feedback,* because if followers are committed to a task, and it is not working or it is difficult, they will respond readily to being shown what is wrong and what will work better. This makes it easier for followers to sign on to a program of change. After this approach comes *reasoning*: If differences are abstract and not apparent to a follower, reasoning can frequently get him or her to conceive the dynamics of a situation in such a way that it makes sense to do what the leader is asking. Thus a union leader may get followers to change their mindset and to temper their demands for immediate gains in contract negotiations by showing that, if granted, their gains would cause them all to lose their jobs because increased costs would force their employer out of business.

Last in the sequence comes *teaching*, that is, education that gets people to slowly learn to see the need for new approaches to problems, to appreciate the need for new mindsets that will generate productive processes, to discover how outdated mindsets may be interfering with responding to a call for change, and to take the personal steps of learning to incorporate new mindsets. As the world has moved away from authoritarian rule and leadership, towards democratic and humanitarian patterns, the approach of "leadership through teaching" has become increasingly important. It is becoming ever more necessary as we continue to build the social organism as a complex of intangible and abstract but very influential sociobiological forces. It takes education, for example, to get farmers to stop using insecticides that immediately boost their crops and profits—but cause an increase in death rates by cancer in the population that eat their products. It takes education to get workers who have been trained to work as a physical machine to learn that even in their role as a simple worker they have the ability, the responsibility, and the right to participate in maximizing the quality of operations of their company.

ADJUST TO FOLLOWERS

So, leaders' approaches evolve to fit their mindsets, as do followers' responses. In order to develop a new leadership approach—for instance, an approach that would rank *teaching* as first in the sequence of changing follower mindsets, and *threats* last—leaders must first adjust their programming, that is, they must develop new mindsets much as did the boy visiting the South and experiencing the black widow spider, and much as I had to do when I arrived at the University of Minnesota in order to find a way to fit into reality as defined by my teachers and my peers.

Let's take a most common and important instance of mindset change that is now called for by our culture. Almost every leader who tells a follower what to do, automatically and unthinkingly assumes that it is his order that controls the outcome. It does not. *Effective action will be forthcoming only if the person receiving the order chooses to do as he or she is told.*

The reality every leader faces is that all behavior is controlled by the mind; furthermore, *the only person who can control a mind is the one who possesses that mind.* A leader may influence a follower's mind, but will not be able to guarantee that the follower will obey an order. Obedience to, or neglect of, the order is the follower's choice only.

Imagine the following scenario: Mr. Jenkins, the owner and CEO of a manufacturing company, tells Mr. Smith, the new vice president of manufacturing, to convert the operation from a top-down authoritarian mode to a participative format that empowers employees and fosters a stronger sense of responsibility for quality at lower levels of the organization.

Mr. Smith, a recently hired, dynamic, motivated, and accommodating employee, sets out to change the program enthusiastically and expeditiously. Mr. Jenkins feels pleased with himself for being such a good manager.

If, however, he could trade places with Clive Williams, CEO of a competing company, he might have to revise his reflections. Mr. Williams does not own the company. His vice president is the nephew of the owner who lives some distance away and who does not interact much with the business. When Mr. Williams gives orders for the same changes as are occurring in his competitor's operation, Jeff, the owner's nephew, resists and flounders because he believes that letting go of tight control is risky and because he knows his uncle is not likely to let him be fired. The program does not move and

Mr. Williams is more or less stuck with his inefficient vice president—and realizes that his giving orders is not what produces results. It is the follower's decision to follow the orders that finally leads to accomplishing the task.

Leaders who decide to include management of the expression of consciousness in their approach must concern themselves with more than simple awareness: they must also look at unawareness. Here, I am not speaking of simple unawareness of the unknown beyond our ken, but of unawareness of the contents of our own consciousness that lie hidden in our subconscious. It sounds perplexing, doesn't it, to speak of being "unaware of consciousness"? This, however, is an important, though paradoxical, truth. Consciousness is a force that energizes our lives—even when we are unaware of it. Our consciousness operates both in awareness and in unawareness.

As you may by now have come to appreciate, whatever happens in an individual's body will find its reflection or parallel in the social body; awareness and resistance to awareness are no exceptions.

What I call the higher self, or inner being, might also be called the *being-consciousness, the totality of the individual.* It is the function of *mind* to serve that being by transforming its aliveness, its consciousness, into life experience. Actions initiated by mind, therefore, become *expressions of being-consciousness.* In an enlightened person the mind does this within a state of awareness that includes supra-consciousness. However, a mind can operate without awareness of any consciousness beyond itself, beyond mind-awareness of mind. It can operate without awareness of any connection between its mind-consciousness and the supra-consciousness energy from which it arises and of which it is a part. In fact, mind can believe that it is the being and that its mission is to serve itself (its set of ideas or pattern of thought). Such mode of operation is the *ego state* of mind where the mind is "I." In any moment, the mind uses its portion of consciousness to process information and produce experiences of aliveness in mind-consciousness, experiences of aliveness that we call self-*awareness*.

In daily living, the contents of awareness may be called the *conscious mind*. At times when the mind is focusing on stimuli coming from the outside world, it may be aware of what it is experiencing without being aware of its own consciousness, let alone being aware of the force of supra-consciousness from which its energy derives.

Nevertheless, consciousness, as the energy of aliveness, continues to operate both in awareness and in unawareness. While focusing attention on certain information, thoughts, feelings, or impressions, the mind may be unaware not only of consciousness (i.e., the sense of being a being) but also of vast amounts of memories and beliefs built upon past experiences. The contents of such unawareness may be called *unconscious mind*, or the subconscious mind. When the mind is accepting awareness of the higher self, or the inner self, it is in a state of *being-consciousness,* or supra-consciousness, which includes a sense of identity with something larger than one's physical body, a sense of oneness with the universe, with God.

The alert reader will recall how in Chapter Three, I spoke of a baby's being born into the world equipped with full supra-consciousness. That is to say, as an infant, we are completely open to, and responsive to, our own aliveness as a human being. Then we "grow up," and most of us tune our minds into outside influences and draw back from our original awareness of our being selves; we pay much more attention to the world around us, including our own physical person, than we do to what is going on in the depths of our being. We start acting differently from how we behaved as a free and joyous infant; we start "looking out for ourselves," taking care of our ego needs, including copying behavior of others if that seems to be the safest course.

The Defensive Operations of the Mind

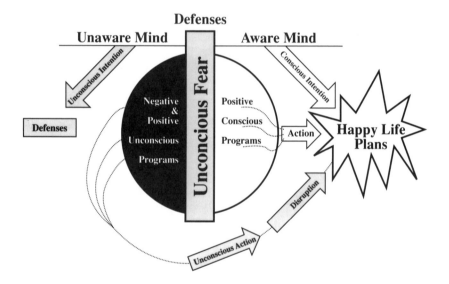

As individuals build their personalities in this fashion, they quickly perceive aspects of the outside world that threaten the image they seek to project. They therefore create individually formed patterns of defensiveness. Here I am not talking about the fright a person might feel if a real tiger were suddenly to leap at him. Such threats are comparatively rare. Instead I am referring to threats against the "image of self" a person has formed in his or her mind. People learn that terrifying psychological experiences that challenge the validity of the images they have created for themselves can be removed by repressing them into the unconscious mind. That is, the mind pushes them "out of existence" by submerging them in unawareness. It is in this fashion that I said the general pattern is for a person to move from the infant's supra-consciousness, to a state of ego-mind-awareness, and then, finally, to the state of predominantly program awareness. In this last stage, the person enters into a life largely dominated by automated mind operations.

Remember, also, how a baby is prepared to accept everyone unconditionally, no matter what their color, age or ethnic or religious background. The baby wants only to be held, smiled at, touched—given attention. Later, as a child, the same person notices differences and places himself in certain niches, according to race, religion, social status or some other peer group. He then distinguishes himself from others, which helps him create a sense of identity (*This is who I am, and this is who I am not.*) Finally, as an adult, the person becomes much more firmly set into a notion of who he is (and isn't). He may then be prone to either smugness or bigotry, if he exalts himself over others, or to self-denigration, if he considers his identity inferior to that of others around him.

"Growth," for such a person, is a matter of recapturing that original supra consciousness of infancy, that marvelous state of freedom that the individual lost by letting his true being be overwhelmed and submerged under a system of defensive attitudes and behaviors designed to protect the ego. The reemergence of early life awareness, that opening up to new possibilities, to higher levels of love, to trust, to tolerance, and to generosity, is a powerful catalytic force for growth

LEVELS OF CONSCIOUSNESS

To help gain a better understanding of the nature of a human being, let us look at being-consciousness in terms of three different levels of expression, *each of which may operate in either awareness or unawareness.* The three levels are:

1. Conscious Mind
2. Unconscious and/or Subconscious Mind
3. Being-Conscious and/or Supra-Consciousness.

For most people, the latter two states are what we call the unconscious; it is important to note, however, that while they are "out of awareness," they are nevertheless an important part of our operating self and they affect us powerfully.

CONSCIOUS MIND

The "self," or what I experience as "me, myself, and I," we should remember, is much more than what we choose to be aware of consciously. It consists of all the programs, mind tapes, operations, and perceptions that we are, or can be, aware of—plus everything that is going on deep inside ourselves that we keep outside our awareness.

In highly program-aware individuals, consciousness may usually be limited simply to awareness of immediate sensory data and the mind programs operating on those data.

More aware individuals, those in ego-mind-awareness, may experience quite an expansion of conscious material. The expansion can include awareness of their own programs (or tapes) and of their capacity to make adjustments to them, or even to shake free altogether from certain tapes in order to behave differently. In short, they may be aware of their ability to be free of constraints previously imposed by their minds.

If awareness extends to "being-consciousness" (or "supra-consciousness"), an individual experiences a deeply felt, intuitive, sense of being connected to universal consciousness, God, the harmony of the universe.

UNCONSCIOUS OR SUBCONSCIOUS MIND

Let me make an important distinction: awareness is the part of consciousness to which a person pays attention. Unconsciousness is another part of consciousness, which has activity, motion, and impact, but to which the person does not pay attention. Unconsciousness, in other words, is not simply "non-consciousness;" rather, it is consciousness that resides in us, but of which we have chosen to make ourselves unaware. The unconscious is a "something," not a "nothing," and it has potent impact upon how we live our lives.

Unconscious mind is made up of two kinds of programs that by definition are not in awareness. One set is truly unconscious because they are so much a part of biology that their mechanisms are not easily noticed in the conscious mind. The brain contains these largely inherited programs that run our body's automatic operations, managing such things as blood flow, brain waves, and organ functioning. With great practice, a person can sometimes become aware of some of these programs, and perhaps may even influence them. For the most part, however, they operate without being available to our attention or control.

Nevertheless, it is important for us to know about these biological programs because, while we may not be aware of them directly, we do affect their operations by the way we manage the conscious and subconscious parts of our minds. A person can, for example, if she keeps herself stressed or depressed, cause her immune system to turn down, or her blood pressure to rise, or her digestive system to go off track. In fact, although most of us seem to be unaware of it, we have power to improve or hinder aspects of health, effectiveness, and bodily operation that are run by mind programs that are out of our awareness.

Subconscious mind, on the other hand, is much more deserving of our conscious attention. It also operates outside our awareness most of the time. But some of its contents are on the borderline of awareness, and they can move in and out of our awareness. Basically there are two kinds of subconscious programs.

The first class of subconscious programs are those we learned so well that we relegated them to unawareness so they could operate comfortably and automatically without further attention or effort. These include such operations as eye-hand coordination, judgment of spacial relationships (seen, for instance, in automatic responses while driving a car, such as shifting gears and stopping for red lights), reactions to perceived dangers, avoidance of disliked foods, and acting out subtle prejudices (such as turning away from panhandlers or avoiding looking directly at severely handicapped individuals).

The second class of subconscious programs are those we learned but subsequently rejected from awareness because they were painful or frightening. This group includes such programs as: "I am not worth loving," "I am not smart," "People who are different from me and my peers are inferior or threatening," " Speaking out in a group will be embarrassing," or "Members of the opposite sex are not to be trusted."

Though they are not in awareness, these programs—the biological, the habitual, and the repressed beliefs about self and others—all continue to churn along inside our minds, focusing consciousness into perceptions and actions according to their prescriptions. They impact whatever parts of our minds and bodies they may happen to tie into.

BEING-CONSCIOUSNESS

Being-consciousness is out of awareness for almost everyone. When it happens to slip into awareness, a person is likely to be overwhelmed by it and have difficulty even talking about the experience. It's difficult to describe or to explain an experience that consists of feeling connected to all other people, to nature, to human history, to the universe, to God. It is a state of consciousness that is inevitably compassionate in flavor. This state of consciousness, which I call supra-consciousness rather than a state of mind (or merely the product of mindsets), is the fundamental state of awareness to which consciousness will return if unobstructed by the mind; it contains all other forms or expressions of awareness.

We might consider this state of consciousness as if it were a deep lake. You may be floating around on top of the lake with a sense that something may be visible beneath and may lend itself to being experienced from the surface. With the right equipment, you might also experience the lake by being in its depths. This experience would be quite different from merely imagining what was beneath the surface.

In this state of plunging into the depths of being, a person comes into a deep knowingness of the powers of his mind and body. He experiences himself as part of God, as one with all life, in a harmonious relationship with everything that exists or has ever existed. This deep sense of cosmic connection to all creatures and all being naturally inclines him to exercise compassion.

Being-consciousness can be experienced in the conscious mind. When it happens, a person may describe himself as having been caught up in a mystical moment or a spiritual experience. Despite the intensity of such experiences, however, this level of consciousness does not have direct operating control over the processes of a person's mind. Rather, this state of supra-consciousness allows him to experience a kind of overview that contains and yet is apart from the mind's awareness of "I" or "myself," just as the sky envelops, but is apart from the earth. Experiencing such an overview imparts a "knowingness" to the mind, which inevitably affects the mind profoundly in its perceptions and intentions. One effect that may be noticed is a realization by the individual of the uselessness of defensive, ego-based reactions. He will also experience a desire to express his consciousness more fully.

MECHANICAL MIND

The mind in a simple state of program-awareness operates mechanically. It records programs, interprets stimuli from the outside world, and then reacts within the limits of those programs. Since the mind's basic function is to insure the survival of the body, and therefore the survival of the being, a mind that is untouched by being-consciousness will inevitably be egocentric in its focus and automatic in its reactions. In essence, the person becomes only his mind and body. Such a condition is not fully human; it leaves the deep inner being either dormant or unexperienced. What is more, this state is antispiritual and generally negative for the person and for the person's interactions with others. Basically, the egocentric person is always fully engaged in defending the rightness and correctness of the mind's positions, which the ego represents. The egocentric individual shapes thoughts and actions to reflect what is right in terms of the mind's programs. He or she always reacts in accord with the physical or emotional conditions that those programs generate within the psyche.

Nine / *The True Enemy: Resistance To Awareness*

How ego operates can be illustrated strikingly by a recent visit of a U.S. congressman to Brazilian officials. He met with them to discuss how Brazil's handling of the rain forest was endangering the earth's atmosphere. The Brazilian group, seemingly blind to global consequences of such acts, reacted with anger over what their mindsets saw as "outside interference" in their nation's sovereignty.[2]

Let's consider the situation of a dispute between labor and management in which the union, coming from its programmed mind awareness, is pushing aggressively for a larger share of the earnings of the corporation. Assume that doing so will probably push the company into a position in which it cannot maintain its market share in the face of foreign competition. The fact that the demands of the union could force the closing of the company may be clouded over by the darkness of the ego position held by the union's negotiating team. The other side of this coin is that, under other circumstances, where there is money to share, management's ego position in defense of maximizing dividend returns to the owners can greatly overshadow the possibilities of allotting a greater share to the employees.

These kinds of interchanges become ego battlefields. There are many other social situations and responses that indicate how much our world is shaped by mechanical program mindsets—mindsets that support self-serving egos, rather than mindsets open to the influence of the spiritual being. The list is long: widespread crime in our society, police abuse on the streets, international drug production and trafficking, the breakdown of family life, escalating mental-health problems, and on and on.

Most of our world has been created by minds oriented towards win/lose competitiveness, fear of scarcity, perspectives of being weak or being strong, of being right or being wrong, of being good or being bad, them and us, mine and yours: in other words, from attitudes of acquisitiveness, control, and dominance. These are typical operations of minds devoid of the spiritual leavening that arises from being consciousness.

Much flawed leadership is a product of negative, subconscious processes. For example, an apparently strong and confident leader may, as a result of unhappy experiences in his childhood, unconsciously believe that he is weak and incompetent. In resistance to that belief, he may develop rigid needs to be right. He may, therefore, always be on the alert for signs that subordinates do not respect him. Also, he will likely see such signs in very insignificant occurrences. He nitpicks his decisions and aims for impossible perfection, thereby blocking out most creative approaches to problem solving.

This leader may overcontrol others and react so negatively to criticism that no one will risk giving him productive feedback. Despite the fact that his attitude causes him to lose out on promotions, and does not motivate his subordinates, he will internally defend his counterproductive behaviors as "necessary." He will say things such as, "You've got to lay down the law; you can't be shilly-shallying around with the rules and regulations." To such a leader, the beliefs that he or she has internalized, and now constantly defends through rationalizations, appear to be perfectly logical and valid.

Many people who have buried their fears of inferiority or insecurity in their unconscious minds turn into workaholics who cannot spend leisure time with their families. They are overconcerned with right and wrong, and they are too critical of themselves and others. Some are unduly competitive.

Furthermore, individuals who unconsciously evaluate themselves in some negative fashion often project those negatives onto others around them. Those who see themselves as unlovable, unworthy of approval, respect or acceptance, tend to shut themselves off from normal human relationships in order to fend off fear of painful rejection. In such a case the individual may feel anger and resentment toward those whom he is shutting out. This person subtly rationalizes: "There is nothing wrong with me; *they* are the ones with the unfriendly attitude."

Far too many people rely on these defense mechanisms, perpetually thinking and acting irrationally. Since these mechanisms are generalized to the social mind, they are the well-spring of society's unending flow of neuroses, psychoses, depression, unhappiness, hypertension, high-blood pressure, impotence, boredom, and who knows what else. They generate the work load for psychiatrists, psychologists, social workers, the police force, and other mental health professionals. They contribute significantly to the occupancy of many psychiatric hospitals and wards. They also contribute to the spread of crime, war, terrorism, and the kind of righteousness that always makes the other person out to be "wrong."

This widespread subconscious system of strongly defended fears and beliefs has direct and important impact on leaders and on society. It shapes corporate cultures, communities, religious denominations, university atmospheres, and even national character. If large portions of a population are trained to cultivate such negative subconscious beliefs, the social mind breaks out in the same neurotic excesses that individuals do. Extreme examples of such outbreaks are the Ku Klux Klan, Neo-Nazi Skinheads, militia and survivalist colonies, and urban street gangs. And, as the product of depressed, hopeless mindsets, we may count many of the urban poor trapped in ghettoes or shabby housing, rural poor living in broken-down trailers or shanties, and the homeless who rifle trash cans in search of food.

More generalized in the American social fabric is a neurotic and excessive consumerism. The subconscious belief in a "need" to have the latest thing causes people to be dissatisfied with what they have and to discard perfectly sound automobiles in order to have the "latest model." Also, the extreme sense of discomfort felt by some if their clothes are slightly out of style is surely based upon a submerged sense of personal inadequacy. Some people are victims of corporate culture workaholism that makes executives feel guilty if they work less than sixty hours a week.

A common product of such mindsets is a win/lose orientation, which may make sense in football or basketball, but has a sharply negative impact on the quality of our lives in general. It may account for the tendency in politics to shape issues for partisan victories rather than to achieve the best solution for the body politic.

Leaders are no less human than anyone else. They, too, live under the control of their negative and subconscious beliefs and fears, however much they may believe their conscious minds are in charge. Therefore, they bring to their leadership everything that is inside of them, that which is conscious and that which is not, that which supports their intentions and that which interferes with them. Usually, with little or no awareness that they are doing it, they project into their workspace their unconscious angers, fears, suspicions, hurts, resentments, anxieties, self-doubts, and more. Their peers and their subordinates catch the full brunt of the leader's submerged negative memories and beliefs. Leaders, in effect, may not be dealing with a situation as it really is, but rather only as they perceive it through the filter of their wounded egos.

Leadership by such people will be chronically off-target. It will be interlaced with emotional crises that are really their own creation rather than complications arising out of situations. Subconscious fears may cause this kind of leader to be too cautious, and buried anger may cause him to be too quick to blame or criticize. Unconscious fear of rejection may cause a leader to be too slow to discipline or to provide negative feedback because he fears that such actions on his part might provoke anger or rejection from the subordinates. The consequence of this kind of impasse may be chronic inefficiency in an operation.

Followers, of course, also operate under control of subconscious pressures of varying strengths. They add their own negatives to relationships with their leaders and with each other. These forces, interacting with those of the leader, cause an amazing proportion of the actions of a given group to veer away from implicit or explicit purposes or goals. Instead of bearing down on the real problems in a purposeful manner almost everybody gets swept away in a whirlwind of ego-defending or playing-out of emotions triggered by conflicts among personalities in the group.

One of the ways that followers inadvertently weaken leadership is by withholding negative reactions to their leader's performance. "Followers should know," Max DePree warns us, "that they sabotage the entire organization by protecting the leader. Eliminate that fatuous phrase 'no problem' for there *are* problems, and leaders exist to do hard work and be accountable for solutions to hard problems. A leader can only do her best in a truth-telling climate."[3]

In efforts to counter negative, subconscious forces, both leaders and followers often shift into overdrive with their positive impulses. In other words, they revert to hurtful force or compulsion. There may be too much need to win, too great a concern over being right, too much quest for power. The qualities that make for success, productivity, and creativity can all be exaggerated, with clearly negative consequences for the unit and for individuals within it.

Civilization could gain immensely if leaders were aware enough to take the pains to help people recognize and deal with their unconscious, negative mindsets. It is perfectly possible, for example, for us as a society to create in our educational system a thrust toward awareness, toward an avoidance and removal of negative, self-destructive beliefs and self-images, both conscious and unconscious. An effort such as this could very well attenuate much of the hurtful impact these destructive beliefs now have upon the minds of young citizens.

More specifically, subconscious negatives affect everything a person sees and does. Therefore, all leaders, especially, should undergo training to help them become aware of those parts of their personalities that shape their style of leading. The psychological technology needed for providing such training is now available. Our whole society would benefit if leaders took advantage of such training.

---

1. Gardner, John W., *Self-Renewal: The Individual and the Innovative Society*, NY: W.W. Norton & Company, 1981, p5.
2. This elaboration by Paul Kennedy may be helpful: "Yet the destruction is such that by the year 2000 three quarters of the tropical

forests in the Americas may been felled. When, in 1988, satellite photos showed the extent of the burning, followed closely thereafter by news of the murder of union organizer Francisco Mendez (who had tried to prevent ranchers from destroying the forest), a U.S. Congressman supported the idea of putting pressure on Brazil —for example, by opposing international funds for a highway through the forest. This transformed the issue into one of north-south politics: Brazilian officials angrily pointed out that North Americans had not halted the destruction of their own forests over the past three centuries, that Brazil intended to develop its economy as any temperate economy would, and that, in any case, U.S. citizens use fifteen times more energy than Brazilians. Before preaching to others, America ought to set a better example." Kennedy, Paul, *Preparing for the Twenty-First Century,* NY: Random House, 1993, p. 119.

3. DePree, Max, *Leadership Jazz,* NY: Doubleday,1992, p. 205.

Chapter Ten

LEADERS AS SERVANTS

We have always known that heedless
self interest was bad morals; we know now
that it is bad economics.

—Franklin D. Roosevelt

Few leaders, other than some professional politicians, tend to see themselves as servants. Rather, operating out of normally strong egos, they see themselves as someone in control —the boss, the achiever. They are even apt to see their followers as the servants. They give themselves permission to use other people for their purposes in order to get products out the door or to gain other successes they seek in their domains. If most leaders disclosed their actual motives openly, they would probably sound something like this: "I want to be the chief executive because it satisfies my ego; it allows me to be creative; it gives me power and status; it allows me to be productive; it makes me rich; it allows me to show how good I am and what I can do." Few would answer, "It gives me an opportunity to serve."

There is nothing wrong with ego-based motives in and of themselves, so long as they are constrained within the larger framework of serving the greater good of society. Without that overall moral, ethical, and perhaps spiritual guiding constraint, however, individuals are inclined to shape their role and employ their resources primarily to serve self-interests. Nowadays many leaders talk about the servant aspect of their roles, but relatively few seem to base their leadership tactics on that concept. In my experience, the spirit of servanthood more clearly determines administrative concepts practiced in the American military than it does in most other institutions of the nation.

Doctors, nurses, social workers, and teachers are other examples of professionals who, in ideal terms, spend themselves daily for the sake of those who receive their services. Yes, some of these people earn a good living in their chosen fields, especially surgeons and other medical specialists. Nonetheless, there is nothing inherently wrong with being well paid for years of expensive training, and for still more years of experience in the operating room or in critical-care situations. The point is that the focus of their professional lives, as a rule, is upon service to their clients.

I don't see any problem with top leaders also earning large salaries and receiving big bonuses. Being a leader is a terribly demanding and difficult task. It's hard to learn how to do it right. If society is not going to make it personally rewarding to lead, who's going to bother? On the other hand, there *is* a problem if leaders determine their policies principally along the lines of what will maximize their own personal gain, rather than along the lines of how they can best serve their clientele—which by the way, includes their followers.

Politicians typically cast themselves as servants of the public and do indeed exert considerable effort to find out, through polls and other means, what their constituents want, and seek to deliver in kind. Cynicism aside, in many instances politicians understand their role as public servants and they act accordingly. Even those who may have abused check-cashing privileges at the House of Representatives Bank, or those who may be guilty of sexual misconduct, have in countless other situations acted to serve their constituents' interests. At the very least, all politicians are conscious that their constituents are counting on them to behave in a servant fashion. Still in all, and regrettably, many politicians pay only lip service to the notion of servanthood while they behave mainly in support of their own interests, of their own intentions, and of their own survival in well-paid, high-status roles.

In the business world, the notion of service as a primary function of leadership has been much less developed, although the idea has been taking on more importance in the past few years. Too many business leaders still have a win/lose orientation. Often what they mean by "winning"—maximizing profits or values of shares—ends up costing employees their jobs or dignity and depriving customers of value and reliability in the products and services they receive. Sadly, many of these excesses in business are generated by leaders to bolster their prestige or to fatten their wallets. In many cases, the blindness to servant responsibility of a leader's role is not simply a matter of selfish or uncaring intentions; rather, it is a function of our society's failure to furnish appropriate training to imbue leaders with the moral compass and ethical perspective they should have to guide them in their work. Therefore, although they do stay within the bounds of the tenets of morality and humanistic concern common to our culture, they are not even aware of the special and more stringent guidelines that ought to apply to their work in light of its significance to the social body.

Too many ego-driven leaders push their subordinates thoughtlessly or even ruthlessly to achieve, achieve, achieve—often mostly for the sake of the leader's own prospects for promotion or merit increases, or demands of ego. When they respond to criticism by arguing that their Machiavellian approaches are justified and ought to be understood as a given in the "real world," they eloquently reveal the vast dimensions of the problem.

RECONTEXTUALIZING

If we want to create a world in which large numbers of leaders truly behave as servants to their employees and customers, we will need to alter some of our controlling social contexts. A context, briefly, is a widely held mindset that forces ongoing situational perceptions, judgments, and conclusions to conform to it. Perhaps the simplest, common example of such a context is a racial prejudice.

Basically I want to promote revisions in the currently held, mostly unconscious, context of leadership. In the past, leaders, when they launched armies into war, were supported by a context of patriotism, love of country, and willingness to lay down one's life for country. Why could they not now be supported by an institutionalized spirit of leadership as servanthood to heal and preserve our human society?

A context, once again, is a sort of master mindset regarding a particular aspect of the world. It consists of many beliefs, attitudes, and expectations working together to shape what we see and how we respond to it. In one context, a male executive may have the old-fashioned, machismo view of the roles of men and women in society and in business. Guided by a different context, another male executive may regard the social roles of men and women as a matter of choice, with both genders equally qualified to play the game of business. When faced with a choice between men and women for a high-level executive position, these two contexts would lead to very different perceptions, judgments, conclusions, and actions.

I call the transformation needed to establish the leader role as a service function "recontextualizing." There are many examples of this process in our history. Imagine the momentous changing of context that was necessary for the colonists in America to break from the Crown and found a democracy 4,000 miles from England's shores. As daring as they were resourceful, the founding fathers endorsed a document which says that all human beings are created equal and have inalienable rights to life, liberty, and the pursuit of happiness. These were truly revolutionary ideas, considering that the colonists had disembarked in the New World as loyal subjects of a British monarch.

Einstein, with his theory of relativity, created an entirely new context for physics, a context that rendered nil much of what had previously been considered the "truth." Civil rights legislation in the United States mandated integration of schools, restaurants, and public transportation, and promoted universal suffrage, leading to the election of numerous African-Americans and Latinos to key government posts. More recently, people tore down the Berlin Wall, and communism collapsed. Apartheid and minority white rule in Africa dissolved. Each is a result of a recontextualization in the social mind.

Until recently, the context for leadership decisions in our society has been unduly influenced by attention to demands rising from various parts of the social body for short-term, localized relief or improvement. In most cases, those making the demands have been fairly oblivious to the impact on the whole society of what they are demanding for themselves. Tobacco growers want to keep their federal subsidies even in the face of federal campaigns to stop smoking. Ohio rejoices that a consolidation of military bases in the continental United States means a net gain for Ohio despite a loss for many other regions. And the "I'll-scratch-your-back-if-you-scratch-mine" ethic on Capitol Hill has ballooned the federal budget with numerous pork-barrel projects.

In addition, our society continuously rationalizes and projects in order to make whatever goes on in the world fit its view of the universe. Rather than solving problems by doing what is required, we change what we "see" to fit what we already believe, that is, to fit the logic of our narrow self-interests. So we do what fits our minds rather than what fits the problem. For example, in the criminal justice system, despite the fact that the prison system does not, in the main, rehabilitate criminals, and in fact may even train them to be more effective criminals, we continue to seek to manage crime by locking people up in subhuman conditions. In other words, we fit our actions to a peculiar logic that we can avoid crime if we can simply get the criminals off the street. Never mind that the way we do it may tend to reinforce their criminal natures, and that a large percentage of those convicted of crimes will sooner or later return to the streets anyway.

Somehow we are coming from an inappropriate context that shapes our view of this problem. Our approach is based too much on program-awareness, too little on ego-mind-awareness and even less on supra-consciousness. And thus we go round and round ratifying the same outmoded hypotheses, and committing many of the same mistakes.

To the extent that the world's leadership-element operates from program-awareness, leadership will sustain the status quo, whether or not that is what reality calls for. Leaders create the reality they believe, and then they believe the reality they have created. As the intelligent reader can now imagine, to a sometimes frightening extent we let ourselves be run by automatic social reflexes that no longer serve us well. We do so without realizing that we have the power to override these mechanisms and to respond differently. Much of the leadership-lag occurs because of the "discontinuous change" that Charles Handy described in his book *The Age of Unreason*.[1] Such changes catapult us into a new situation for which we find ourselves unprepared. We flounder and make false starts because our mindsets are stuck in an outmoded reality, and we have not yet adapted to the new reality.

Leadership Lag

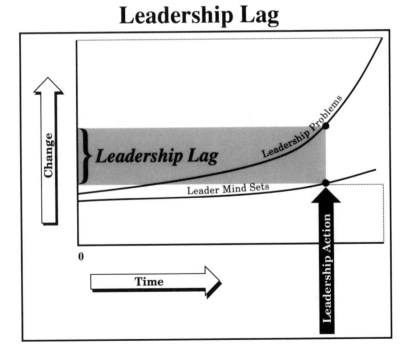

As a consultant to industry, I have seen firsthand the pervasiveness of the reflex and control mechanisms that are built into our authority structures. New complexities of industrial operations necessitate a radically different approach in order to involve human minds and energies in the production process. However, moves to supplant the tradition of authoritarian leadership in large corporations often lead to upheavals because both leaders and followers continue to view things through their old mindsets.

Still, by moving through the process of increasing awareness, from program-awareness to ego-mind-awareness and, perhaps, to supra-consciousness, awkward and painful though it may be, both bosses and followers can find themselves transformed. They develop a new context. Once transformed into advocates of something like "participative management," they would be hard put to retreat to the old authoritarian structures. The new policies and modes of operation, once put into effect, take on a life of their own and become the context of a new reality.

The same must be attained more widely in our world. We need social transformation despite the pains and chaos that transformation will bring. We need to scuttle the dusty old mindsets of the past and highlight mindsets adapted to present conditions. To create this transformation will require a great deal of new leadership.

For example, most leaders of our school systems now operate within a general context that says all students should be given the same form and level of education. This context judges it inappropriate to design a school system on the assumption that some students have intellectual makeups that make them incapable of absorbing the full force of current educational programs. On the other hand, some students may be able to absorb even more if it is offered to them. Yet, in the current context, it is considered unacceptable to designate such differences and to teach students according to their ability. That context does not take into account the possibility that our culture would be a great deal healthier and happier if individuals were educated to be all they are and can be—and to be satisfied and happy with that.

DOING WHAT'S NEEDED, NOT WHAT EVERYONE WANTS

So, you are not necessarily performing as a good servant leader just because you listen to what people say they want, and then arrange to give it to them. A key function of leadership, in fact, is being able to see what is needed for the good of the whole more clearly than the people you are leading, and seeing how to achieve the goal more clearly than they do. Very often the essence of leadership turns on leading people not to where they want to go, but to where they need to go for their own stated purposes. Progress frequently results from leaders taking unpopular positions, something that Adlai Stevenson spoke about during his bid for the presidency in 1954. [2]

It is lazy leadership to act simply to please followers regardless of what, in the long run, will really serve their purposes. Though your leadership behavior may please them at the time, they will reject you in the end when they discover that your overly accommodating style of leadership has not achieved desired goals. Supra- conscious leadership involves being willing to go up against your followers' resistance and to motivate them to do what is good for them, in spite of contrary desires on their part. Supra-conscious leadership, for instance, continues to work hard to curtail the slaughter of whales despite the fact that such curtailment is strongly resisted by those who profit from killing whales.

Weak leaders just want to please those around them at all times. They are too hungry for acceptance, or too unwilling to buck resistance or rejection. Or they just don't want to anger anybody, which would mean spending energy to deal with angry people. Though I do not condone weak or lazy leadership, as described above, I do understand the conditions that produce it, for leadership is a perilous affair.

A leader who acts too assertively on his beliefs about the greater good may propose approaches that will be seen as immediate losses by his followers, who will not respond. Or, the leader will become a "benevolent dictator" for the "good of his followers." Obviously, such an approach is not a proper road in a democracy. The problem, therefore, is to lead in a way that uses democratic processes to get people to decide to change their minds and to create a new context, and then to participate in identifying the greater good.

Leaders have learned—even though most of them have not been able to articulate it in this way—that their power is on loan to them from their followers. Therefore, the price of keeping power becomes doing what followers will accept. Quite naturally, then, the mindset of the leadership-element focuses on understanding, anticipating, satisfying, conforming to, or manipulating the demands issuing from followers. In a slowly changing society, this tendency generally supports the needs and freedoms of followers. However, under the conditions of explosive change with which we are now confronted, this reactive mode of leadership generates "leadership-lag." And that means that we let problems mass and overwhelm us before we try to concoct and set in motion appropriate new solutions.

A more basic difficulty arises. Leaders attempting to please followers will not even attempt to move their organizations beyond outmoded mindsets which may be causing problems faced by the organization. But the world now needs leaders who will *take it away from the known*, into unfamiliar and sometimes psychologically new conditions that are called for if we hope to keep up with the evolutionary trends of the globe. Thus, for example, the heavy focus on productivity and consumerism that has powered our free enterprise engine and created our current standard of living may have to be abated if we are to avoid exhausting the limited resources of the planet.

Leaders who have fortitude, foresight, and an attitude of service must seek to acquire the tact needed to lead wisely, for it will take both courage and tact to negotiate an effective change with followers who are fixated on short-term, personal gain, and who view the world through mindsets that are behind the times.

The leadership problem at this point is to proactively get followers to build new and adaptive mindsets. In our time, this is the clearest and most demanding job of supra-leadership that we face.

---

1. Handy, Charles, *The Age of Unreason,* Boston: Harvard Business School Press, 1989.
2. What Stevenson actually said was: "All progress has resulted from people who took unpopular positions." Speech, March 22, 1954, Princeton University. While I do not go so far as to agree with his notion of "All progress resulting from taking unpopular positions," it is clear that the leader who avoids unpopular positions is unlikely to generate any progress.

Chapter Eleven

PROFESSIONALIZING LEADERSHIP

*The winds and waves are always on
the side of the ablest navigator.*

—Edward Gibbon

The need to professionalize the leadership role is upon us. This means not only deeper and more formal training for leaders, it also means the instituting of professional organizations and ethical standards, and peer review—just as we have had for generations of doctors and lawyers.

Without much fanfare during the past decade, a handful of academic programs in leadership have evolved. One may be able to earn an advanced degree in leadership, but the opportunity is not widespread. Although the emergence of such programs is an encouraging sign, the degree most often sought by would-be leaders is still that of business administration, where, typically, the emphasis falls on the managing of nonhuman systems rather than on leading people.

This emphasis needs to be changed. If you have absorbed the lessons of this book thus far, you already understand why. The central reason that impels us to professionalize leadership is that we are undergoing, whether we like it or not, whether we even *know* it or not, a fundamental change from a world of independent task-leadership constructs to a world of *necessarily interdependent* supra-leadership constructs.

Far back in history when the world was simpler and social units were smaller, leadership needs were usually simple, direct, and obvious, and they were met in the natural flow of things. As we moved into our present era of complex social units and industrialization, we began doing more "management" than leadership. Much of that management came out of engineering or accounting, and involved principally the handling of machinery and money. People were treated like equipment, cogs in a machine, or as a line item on a profit and loss statement. If I was in charge of a public unit or a company, what I did seemed to have little effect on the rest of the world. We continued to lead based on the age-old notion that if you just took care of your own backyard, you and your people would make enough money and have a decent life. And the backyards were *not* seen as interdependent.

Those traditional mindsets developed in a world that appeared to be, at root, radically independent—the independence of the pioneers. Did you want to "get ahead"? The counsel you probably received was, "*Do it yourself. Pull yourself up by your own bootstraps.*" We lived thus immersed in the old bootstrapping school of "rugged individualism," and we prided ourselves upon mastering it. Everybody was supposed to "take care of yourself" (The '90s version of this, born from the terrible phenomenon of drive-by shootings, is the expression "Watch your back!") When I first worked with leaders in corporations and in public entities, my clients asked me and my staff to solve people problems as if human beings were simply equipment in the organizational setup. Clients were trying to maximize by using our psychotechnology to make people more productive. "Doctor, please increase the flow-through of energy in our people," was a common request. In essence we were asked to train people so they could put out more for the company. Or we were asked to screen applicants for positions as if they were a piece of equipment, not a person with feelings, ideas, and a family history.

Given the mindsets of the time, this approach was understandable. But there was an error in it. It was this: companies were putting scarcely any attention into the quality and effectiveness of the human side of the equation. The fact that people were not, indeed, "just machines," was not considered. As a behavioral scientist, I began to focus on the aspect of leadership that had to do with understanding and applying the volitional human capacities that take care of the problems of organization or machinery. That quickly led me to see that the machine side that clients thought made such a difference was basically a product of *people*. By fine-tuning the people input into technology, you could get a much better flow on the production line. That is what the Japanese figured out long before we got around to it, and that is one reason they became so admirably efficient as producers.

I also saw that leaders tended to shoot for immediate goals and not really think in terms of overall goals for the larger units of which they were a part (division, company, industry, region, country, world). When they ran into trouble, as frequently they did, they found that they did not know how to interrelate systems. How, for example, do you get Marketing and Research and Production and Sales into a relationship where they automatically have the synergy needed to create a system in healthy balance? Even more fundamentally, how do they at least create a system in which they can understand each other and communicate clearly?

Often, they simply did not have adequate communication channels or structures. And if they did, egos got in the way. This caused them to spend too much of their energy vying with each other for company perks instead of working together to achieve synergy.

A third observation I made was that leadership tended toward a shortsighted view of the future. Long-term goals received scant attention, as did the inevitable problem of interrelating goals with other departments or with other units of society. *The result often was that the activities of the various parts ended up diminishing the quality or the effectiveness of the whole.*

If we keep on with each leader minding only his or her own unit's affairs, nobody noticing what other leaders are doing, few people attempting to integrate their actions with those of other leaders, we eventually will generate terrible diseases in our social body. And if we ruin the organs that are equivalent to the liver or the lungs or the heart, the whole body is going to break down and die. Thus my model of the human body as metaphor for our society. In a similar vein, years ago, I found the best way to approach an ailing corporation was to see it as a neurotic individual. That worked. It still does.

At this point, almost through the last decade of the last century of the second millennium after Christ, we are still struggling to break out of tremendous inertia to keep on doing leadership in all the old, now fatally flawed ways. We are going to need an equally tremendous push on behalf of all aware leaders and followers, such as those of you now working toward the end of this book and nodding in agreement, to institute *training programs* and *professional standards* for present and future leaders.

We need to move a lot of people out of their stultifying program-awareness into ego-mind-awareness and on up the mountain toward supra-consciousness. That process can happen in many different ways, not all of them formalized, but there *are* definite patterns of training that can be set up to facilitate these transitions, and this should, at all costs, be done. Otherwise we are going to remain in a quagmire in which society is really foundering in its old mindsets, making it unable to shake free and create vital new models for to live by in our interdependent world. Society, as my models demonstrates, is an organism, whether we are aware of it or not. And we all belong to it and depend upon its functioning. It is a complex organism of many parts, and the well-being of the whole depends upon how well all of the parts work together. A human body cannot function without a heart. At the same time, the heart cannot function on its own either; it has to derive oxygen from the lungs; blood must flow in and flow out; there must be communication with the brain and with the muscles.

This same interdependency holds true for society, despite the fact that most of us do what we do from the perspective of belonging to a part in society, rather than from the perspective of belong to the *whole*. We are not yet adequately tuned in to the degree to which the health and safety of our individual part of society (family, company, town, etc.) is dependent upon the health and safety of the whole society. *Society's interdependencies are, in effect, the very basis for its operations and its survival.* Failure in any one part of the body can affect all the other parts—even, conceivably, to the point of total destruction of our social body.

SUPRA-CONSCIOUS LEADERSHIP

As all scientists know, any organism lives in a dynamic, synergistic, interactive state. Society definitely lives this way, and this phenomenon of interdependence has in fact been rapidly increasing over the past two hundred years. There is no reason to suspect that we shall not be even more dependent upon one another each passing year as our global population mushrooms and all our technological and economic systems intermesh.

One effect of this increasing interrelatedness is that leadership becomes more and more critical. As our social body grows larger, it needs a more and more sensitive mind and nervous system, through which command and operation of the social body occur. As society or a unit of society such as a corporation or a school gets larger and becomes more bureaucratic, there is more and more need for an integrating structure. This calls for leadership. Leaders are the people who monitor the interactions, who make the decisions, or mandate the actions, who gather, process, and analyze the data, and who do the coordinating.

Members of a symphony orchestra depend upon a conductor to coordinate their instrumentation to produce a sophisticated rendition of a sonata or concerto. Workers in an automobile factory depend upon a supervisor to tie their efforts together and produce a finely tuned engine and tightly welded chassis. What is true of an orchestra or of an automobile plant is even more true of the ever-changing, highly interdependent, organismic and dynamic state of being we call society.

The orchestra conductor must know the score thoroughly, for every instrument, from violins through the woodwinds to the percussions. The supervisor of the production line at Saturn or Toyota must have intimate knowledge of every process on the line and of how the various processes interrelate. At societal levels we need leaders who have similar knowledge of what is being carried out in their domains and who are capable of orchestrating many social processes so that things get harmonized and so that positive outcomes result. Beyond that, as things become more complex, it will also be important that followers—who are close to our systems' operations—acquire more and more knowledge about how things work—and about how they must be fit together.

This ties into the leadership-element, that part of society made up of all leaders, with feedback loops and communications technology and data storage processing. This system serves to determine and guarantee the operating and survival needs of both the parts and the whole of our social body. And the more interdependent society has become, the more the leadership-element has grown in importance *until now it is absolutely vital for the survival of our world.*

In the old days of strictly task-oriented leadership, a leader could, say ninety percent of the time, make independent decisions that did not affect people outside his community. Most of the impact of his leadership was local. Now a leader has much greater and often unrecognized responsibility to the overall leadership-element and its well-being, over and above the well-being of the leader's own particular unit. As things stand today, a great many leaders focused on doing their operations independently of society's intermeshing systems do not realize that, collectively, they are killing the rain forest, or producing a choking layer of pollution in the ionosphere. One man chopping down a tree does not see that he is but one of thousands around the globe doing the same, and that the net result of extreme deforestation will be negative for the planet.

SUPRA-CONSCIOUS LEADERSHIP

What we need today is overriding leadership and directionality to respond to supra-regional or supra-national problems. Since the days of Woodrow Wilson and his dream of linking the nations in a league, we have begun to get some of the structures we need in organisms such as the United Nations, the World Health Organization, the World Bank, NATO, etc. But this is only a beginning. The truth is, we need much more.

A PROFESSIONAL BODY

The leadership-element must operate as a self-conscious body if it is truly to be effective in guiding interactions in our increasingly complex and interdependent world. We will no longer be able to move ahead productively with a majority of leaders who barely understand themselves as leaders at all—thinking of themselves more as "managers"—and who have little or no awareness of the fallout from their operations on the larger units to which they belong. Furthermore, we need to take into account that followers are also part of the leadership-element whose consciousness and performance we want to improve.

To this end, *society needs to professionalize leadership*. For purposes of discussion let us assume we have already done so by creating a standards-setting and review organization called The World Professional Leadership Association (WPLA). As I visualize it, the WPLA is structured as an international body to:

- Oversee the leadership-element as a crucial social institution.
- Create standards of professional ethics and accreditation for leaders.
- Foster the creation of leadership training and development resources in society.

- Develop a reservoir of knowledge on the roles and processes of leadership.
- Foster and conduct research on, and promote awareness of, supra-leadership.
- Foster proactive leadership that supports the evolution of stable, healthy, free, creative, and life-engendering systems for society and the planet.

Readiness is a mindset that harbors a desire to make something happen. If we believe in something strongly enough, our belief will empower us and lead to action. Since our society is a creation of our minds, if we reprogram our minds to conceive of social assumptions and processes differently, and if there are enough of us working together to do it, we can change our social matrix to match our changing reality. As I have said, that reality includes the objective fact of a world of rapidly burgeoning population and of increasingly interdependent systems.

A necessary first step for each person who enrolls in this mission of shaping leadership as a social institution will be to plunge deeply into his or her own soul and develop the self-awareness that is crucial for being able to lead others. This should become an absolute priority for all conscientious leaders. Without sufficient self-awareness, a leader is merely "shooting in the dark"—and may well do more damage than good.

Next, leaders will have to provoke greater awareness in others around them—in other leaders and in all followers. *Everyone needs to be made aware that he or she is an element in a collective body and a force either for sanity or destruction.* There will be no middle ground. Nonetheless, the program of change must be carried out democratically, not through manipulation or force. What we are faced with is a massive program of public reeducation to the realities of our world. This program demands great awareness on the part of educators, coupled with warmth, compassion, and keen pedagogical skills.

WPLA is conceived as developing into a self-aware, socially responsible nucleus of a worldwide leadership-element. An initial task of this body is to define its own role, purpose, and the ethics that will guide its evolution. Of first importance is the consideration of the philosophical commitment to the support and protection of individual rights and liberties within a commonwealth that strives to promote the greatest good for all human beings. Moreover, the leaders of WPLA must take great care to resist the inevitable temptation to use their power and authority to serve their own narrow interests rather than those of the social body.

As a first priority, WPLA will take the lead in developing research into the social mechanisms and psychology of leadership, and in instituting and evaluating programs of leadership training. In a variety of ways we should weave leadership training into the structures of our entire educational system, from grammar school through the university. This is not something to be reserved simply for students of business or government alone. Self-awareness, understanding of the current state of society and of all useful leadership paradigms must be essential elements of all training. At the highest level, we should expand upon the number of master's and doctoral programs in leadership available today. Indeed, it should pain us that at this writing there are so few degree programs in leadership available anywhere in the world. We devote much more time and money to providing M.A. and Ph.D. programs in subjects of far less social significance than the practice of leadership, without which our society simply cannot continue to operate.

The availability of such training will also be important to followers, because the quality of the leadership they receive will have either positive or negative impact upon the quality of their lives. Besides, most leaders begin by being followers. Followers, of course, are critical to leaders. It is only by studying followership that leaders can learn how they are to develop their skills. Let us recall, too, that it is only by shaping their calls for action according to what will fit the followers' perceptions of reality that leaders will get any followership at all to result. A good definition of leadership, indeed, is this:

LEADERSHIP MEANS MANAGING MINDSETS

As things stand today, many leaders do a lackluster job of managing mindsets. Most are woefully unaware of what goes on in followers' minds. Typically, an unaware leader, focused on goals, creates leadership according to what his own mindset tells him is "right." To him, whatever he believes is "the truth," therefore he unconsciously projects that "truth" onto followers, as if they were naturally supposed to agree with it. (An example would be a case I have already mentioned: that of business leaders who try to get followership from their people by talking up "company growth and increased profits," not realizing that many employees care not a whit for these goals.)

Not only should leaders learn how minds work, they should also have special training in how to map minds—determine, that is, what mindsets each individual is bringing to bear on a situation—and also learn how to communicate with each mind after it has been mapped.

Of course, we still have much work to do to persuade leaders to focus on the human element in their corporate systems. Unhappily, an error still rampant in the work world is to slight people considerations in favor of the nonhuman elements of production—of the technological wizardry. What many leaders still fail to realize is that while it is often true that operating gains from mechanical or technological changes far outweigh their costs to the human side in the short run, in the longer run, the balance shifts. Years of management supporting productivity at the expense of creating dehumanizing boredom for workers has eroded the work ethic. If American workers are less productive than their counterparts in certain other countries, we can assign some of the blame for this gap to management neglect of human dignity, and to management promotion of mind-numbing practices for workers.

Coming full circle, let us recall that everything starts with an understanding of mind and mindsets. All human action is triggered by the mind, and the mind is *totally* under the control of the person who possesses it. Once in place, mindsets tend to be put out of consciousness, placed on automatic, and thereafter cause one to act without making deliberate choices. This automation tends to persist, in inertia, until a jolt of mental/emotional energy brings the mind back to consciousness. For most people, ordinary ongoing conditions do not furnish enough of a jolt. Providing such a jolt, therefore, becomes an important task for aware, proactive leaders who recognize the need to stimulate a change of minds.

TRIGGERS OF SOCIAL CHANGE

For social change to occur there are really only three possible propulsion systems:

> 1. Occasionally, a bottoms-up movement occurs. This could be sparked by dissatisfied workers who band together to form a union and exer-

cise their right to strike. It could be students rallying around a popular teacher that the principal seeks to dismiss. Or it might be residents of a neighborhood who want to head off the nearby siting of a nuclear plant. Leadership will then rise up, ad hoc, from among the participants.

2. Some environmental phenomenon will manifest itself which will force people to take action. Legionnaire's disease may break out in a large assembly, or a river will flood, or word may spread that a child molester is operating in the neighborhood. Such occurrences inevitably provoke people to come together, discuss the situation, and decide upon a course of action.

3. Current leaders themselves, viewing the scene from the vantage point of a lookout or overseer, will perceive that potential problems are taking shape, just as a forest ranger stationed high in a tower can spot the first wisps of smoke that will lead to a devastating forest fire. Then leaders will signal the danger and gather impressions and ideas for solutions from far and wide, and, finally, encapsulate *the best* of what they have learned in a program for change.

If we wait until our social body is so riven with sickness that some environmental catastrophe forces us to act, we are likely to act in haste, with considerable bumbling and some counterproductive shooting off in a scattering of directions.

If we wait until the followers are so frustrated by official inaction that they have to take matters into their own hands, we will have betrayed the public trust and will risk losing our credibility as leaders, exposing ourselves to revolt and rebellion.

The ideal approach to analyzing the conditions of our social body and working to cure festering illnesses and turn the body into a healthy environment for all citizens is for leaders to come together in a fellowship of servants. Yes, there will be much, and probably heated, debate, and many disagreements while our servant-leaders shape policy, and yes, inevitably, some leaders will abuse the trust we vest in them. If, however, significant numbers of caring leaders are recruited to work together for the good of the whole society, we can take tremendous strides in the right direction—and confront and disarm dangers that now threaten our very existence as a global society. In a nutshell, this is the *raison d'etre* behind the professionalizing of leadership. The stakes, as the aware reader can see, are high.

Chapter Twelve

ETHICAL IMPERATIVES

Where there is no vision,
the people perish.
—*Proverbs 29:18*

Attentive readers may have deduced that the term "supra-leadership," as I have used it in this book, refers to leadership of society as a whole, or to leadership of the planet. If this has been your perception, you are on target. However, the term supra-leadership also has a slightly broader connotation. It refers to leadership that is determined by considerations of ripple effects beyond the objectives of an immediate situation. Supra-leadership focuses on the greater good to be achieved in any holistic context—where concentric circles reach out from one unit of leadership to affect an entire division, company, or even a whole industry. They also emanate from that one unit and affect the community in which the unit, such as a company or a public entity, is located. The ripple effects of any leadership action may also impact the wider region and, perhaps, eventually the nation or the world.

Supra-leadership is in force when you are leading for the lesser good (your unit's immediate objectives) in a manner that supports the greater good (the impact on the company as a whole and on the company's surroundings, i.e., the community or the region). What will support the greater good may even be operationally irrelevant to the achievement of your own immediate objectives, but it may nonetheless govern your decision-making.

In many cases, supra-leadership will actually operate to the detriment of your immediate objective. Take the instance of a city's allowing the dumping of garbage in a river. In the short term this seems quite efficient. And cheap. To take care of garbage in other ways, such as by constructing processing plants, costs much more and will necessitate raising people's taxes. In the long run, however, a clean river will make the community a more desirable locus for businesses. It will mean a good and healthful quality of life for the employees. As such businesses grow and pay more taxes, the wisdom of not short-circuiting the region's ecology will become clear.

Let us distinguish between genuine self-interest and greed. Self-interest must take the long term into consideration. Self-interest will promote our own development as humans and the securing of prosperity and peace for ourselves and those others with whom we share this planet. Greed, on the other hand, is usually shortsighted. It is the quick fix type of solution to problems that are complex and full of hidden nettles. It is greed, for example, when the United States considers only its own narrow interests in setting political or socioeconomic policy. We in the United States make up something like five percent of the world's population, yet we consume about twenty-six percent of the world's natural resources to support our lifestyle. Simple logic should tell us that we cannot go on like this forever.

Ultimately, we will have to see that we, just like everybody else, are dependent upon the health of the planet as a whole for our survival. Umberto Eco, the Italian novelist and social thinker, once wrote in a magazine essay that unless Europe paid attention to the marginalized masses of the former Eastern bloc countries, and to the peoples of certain North African states, this underclass would one day simply march into Europe and demand to be taken care of. In the light of California's current concerns about meeting the cost of the social management of its many thousands of illegal aliens, the march may be under way already. Ignoring the marginalized may seem to save resources and energy in the short term. Farther down the road, however, it could be a recipe for disaster. If we are farsighted enough here at home, we will not apply the same logic to the attitudes that the "haves" in the suburbs harbor toward the "have nots" in the ghettoes and in poor rural areas.

There is always a conflict between our desire for immediate gain for our own particular circumstances, and the promotion of the greater good for the wider context in which we live. Greed says, "Give me the quick gain for my immediate satisfaction and to hell with this so-called 'greater good.'" Genuine self-interest says, "No, not so fast. Let's focus on the greater good because, over the years, that is really what will make my life secure and satisfying."

Today, most social contexts still are undergirded by special interest groups working for their own narrow good, often at the expense of the greater good of the social body. These groups operate in a myopic "win-lose" perspective. When people bond together on the basis of these self-serving interests, they tend to create a selfish organizational ethic of "Me first." What we need, rather, are more contexts that serve *all of us in the wider society,* contexts that are truly inclusive.

To redo such contexts proactively, we must consciously, and intuitively, draft statements of purpose that will almost certainly contradict any number of existing societal mindsets. We must start by assuming a context that does not yet exist— the context of a supra-conscious society—and then conceptualize precepts to express its purposes. As we fit purposes, leadership decisions, and actions to the newly assumed context, mindsets will begin to form that gradually will come into closer harmony with the realities of the world as it is currently evolving. What might now be regarded as a rather idealized context will then, one day, begin to operate as a directional force for society. Like all contexts, once it is thoroughly absorbed into our social mind, it will operate automatically as part of our social unconscious.

Supra-national thinking is, of course, not new. The United Nations charter is a manifesto that reflects the spirit of supra-leadership. The Club of Rome's seminal document, *Limits to Growth,* is another. There have been numerous others, drafted by diplomats, social philosophers, economists, and educators. So far, however, these manifestos have not been appreciated and implemented widely enough to change the masses of individual minds that meld together to create our social context. To bring this about we need more than isolated expressions of vision. We need an infusion of aware leadership dedicated to the building of a social mind context that will constantly keep us focused on the supra-effectiveness of whatever we are doing.

In the remainder of this chapter I will lay out a series of tenets for a leadership charter suited to the realities of the world as it is currently evolving. These declarations, and their concrete application, could help us fit purposes and leadership decisions to the new context of global society.

Bearing in mind that the American Declaration of Independence, crafted by Thomas Jefferson, described society's end as assuring each individual the right to "life, liberty and the pursuit of happiness," let us attempt a broad, inclusive statement of purpose for global society.

THE PURPOSE OF WORLD SOCIETY IS TO BE AN INSTRUMENT OF MANKIND, TO SUPPORT HUMAN HAPPINESS AND SATISFACTION, TO NURTURE ALL LIFE ON AND OF OUR PLANET, AND TO SUPPORT THE EVOLUTION OF THE HUMAN SPIRIT TOWARD ITS OWN HIGHEST POTENTIAL.

While an abstract statement points in a direction, or indicates a condition, it does not spell out the specific steps to be taken. A generalized articulation of an ideal context for society may say, "Go West!" but it does not of itself hand us the choice to be made about means of locomotion to use, or which road to take. Nevertheless, at the point of decision an abstract statement of principle serves as a beacon lighting our way; and only the leadership choices that are illuminated by its beam should be considered. Those that lie in the shadows must be rejected.

Holding this abstract declaration in front of us as our objective will create a decision-making bias that will guide efforts to resolve immediate, close-to-home problems in supraconscious ways that simultaneously protect and support the wider social context. The yang force of personal striving would be infused with the yin force of holistic harmony and well-being. That is the desirable bias if we hope to support positive, life-engendering change for our world.

A bias toward holistic decision-making would, ideally, permeate the social body and would militate against many destructive trends in which many people and their leaders now participate, either out of selfishness, ignorance, or lack of adequate consideration of the consequences.

Under the context I am proposing here, government, or "the state," exist "by, of, and for the people," as Abraham Lincoln put it so succinctly. These overarching hierarchies derive their power directly from the electorate and must operate to serve the best interests of that body. Government ought not be "captured" by one or another class of privileged souls, such as the wealthy, or lawyers, or professional politicians. Over and over again in history we have witnessed populations forced into servitude for "the good" of the state's leaders. We have seen nations led into war for selfish purposes—to fuel the arms manufacturing sector, or to relaunch the general economy, or to fulfil the jingoistic fantasies of a powerful few. In some cases "national interests" have been so exaggerated that thousands have laid down their lives for it, even though the only possible "benefits" were boosts to leaders' egos.

Similarly, as I view the broader power structures of our society, such as industrial cartels and "old boy" clubs—those that go beyond the elected or appointed governmental officeholders—I am compelled to say: The presence of a leadership-element that is primarily self-serving to the detriment of the overall good of society must be seen as a neurotic or borderline psychotic condition in the social mind. This condition fosters self-destructive behavior in the social body. As such, this neurosis or psychosis should be identified, countered, and arrested so that the planet and its human systems can become healthy.

Leaders are vital to the process of correcting dangerous aberrations that persist in our social mind, and in reprogramming it to think and to choose in healthier ways. *People today have no option at all as to whether they will follow leaders.* Anarchy is not a viable choice in our highly synergistic, interdependent world. Huge interdependent global operations must be integrated, coordinated, and managed. Complex technical operations require skilled, technical leaders to teach workers what to do. Nations need lawmakers, law enforcers, and administrators of governmental service agencies. In short, our social processes cannot be run without leaders. Therefore, all neurotic and maladaptive behavior by the leadership-element warrants personal and dynamic attention from all of us.

Here is the next statement of ethical principle for the global community:

SOCIAL MIND-SETTING MUST BE MANAGED THROUGH DEMOCRATIC PROCESSES.

The idea of leaders (or unidentified powerbrokers, such as the Trilateral Commission or the Illuminati) deciding what mindsets the general populace should adopt is a threatening violation of personal freedom for intelligent human beings. It is not for leaders alone to decide what mindsets they will ask people to adopt and consult. After all, the only person who can set an adult mind is the person who possesses that mind.

With Lincoln, the poet Walt Whitman, and countless other keen observers of our human condition, I put great stock in the innate wisdom of the common people. Just because most of them are followers and not leaders should not be construed to mean that they do not have sound instincts about what we need to create a sane society. True leaders, indeed, come from the people, respect the people, and stay in careful touch with the people as they work out what they will combat and what they will advocate.

Nonetheless, leaders, by virtue of their position, necessarily have a broader overview of what is going on in society. It is they who can best spot the trends, both the harmful and the helpful ones, and serve as mediators between the popular mind and the councils of government and industry. Therefore, leaders should listen closely, and interpret carefully, the popular wisdom that abounds in society. After careful listening and honest debate, leaders should distill, encapsule in clear expressions, and reflect back to the people the best of what they, the leaders, have been able to learn.

In any event, a corollary to this principle is the following:

THE BASIS FOR CREATING NEW CONTEXTS SHOULD BE SELF-AWARENESS AND UNDERSTANDING, NOT FORCE.

Leaders must not set out to overpower their followers, either by physical force, by threats, by manipulation or by simply steamrollering over the popular will and wisdom. To succeed, therefore, a mind-setting program must begin slowly and take place completely in the open. It should be carried out by leaders and educators who have already carefully thought through their own recontextualizing toward the greater good.

Those most able to facilitate social change will be leaders who have gotten into touch with supra-consciousness, which brings them a sense of harmony with nature and with the universe, and an overall commitment to the greater good of the human experience. They will tend to see that there is no "one way," no one path for all humans to take, but that it is for each person to create his or her own experience within the limits of what will not interfere with others' rights, or with the overall good. In no way does this give even a hint of anarchy. Normal human beings under normal conditions tend to want the same things for themselves and their loved ones. Free of an environment that engenders fear, anger, hurt, defensiveness, and hate, they tend to seek safety, comfort, companionship, enjoyment, challenge, excitement, and love.

There is, in all of this, much room for debate about just what mindsets are the healthiest for our social body. Arriving at such decisions will require the input of all who are willing and motivated to participate.

BOTH LEADERS AND FOLLOWERS NEED TO BECOME SELF-CONSCIOUS ABOUT THE PROCESS OF MANAGING MINDS AND MINDSETS.

Up to now, social mind-setting processes have gone on in largely subconscious fashion, except for a few instances such as developing patriotism and commitments to democracy and, more recently, to civil rights. If truth be known, professionals in the realm of advertising have probably developed more awareness and skill in mind-setting than anybody else. Politicians and certain media magnates probably follow next in line. Lately, so-called "political correctness" advocates have tried their hand at reprogramming people's minds, but with mixed results.

In general, however, as a social body, we have had relatively little practice and have developed only rudimentary skills in the process of mind-setting to create new social contexts. Often, when leaders have attempted to set minds, they have done so awkwardly and badly, in a manner that could not help but generate resistance. Consequently, the products of their efforts have been either fuzzy or negative, and the people have experienced negative feelings about themselves and about their world.

This result can be predicted from knowledge of human nature. We may take as a rule that the quality of our experiences as individuals and as a society is a function of awareness, which, in turn, is a function of our mind's perception of reality. What we experience in ourselves and "out there" in the world is an acting-out of our perception and interpretation of intellectual, psychological, and aesthetic stimuli—let's call it "feedback." This feedback supports and shapes our awareness of and belief in what actually "is." The higher a person's level of consciousness, therefore, the greater his ability to think and act in congruence with what the situation truly demands. Feedback that tells him that he is "on the mark" with his action plans, that the job is indeed being accomplished efficiently—whether the job is to churn out a status report, or to restore a river to ecological health—will go far toward providing him with satisfaction and happiness. Obviously, if leaders suggest views that are discordant with such a person's own perceptions, he will feel confused, or he will rebel.

It is of considerable importance, therefore, that leaders and followers alike stop relying on inadequate, automated mindsets of the past and participate in the deliberate resetting of minds to meet present and future challenges involving work and society.

WE WILL ACHIEVE A HEALTHY BALANCE BETWEEN THE RIGHTS OF THE COLLECTIVE—THE COMMUNITY AS A WHOLE—AND THE RIGHTS OF THE INDIVIDUAL.

The entire history of the United States, and of many other democracies, has been the story of the struggle to achieve just this balance. Things remain in flux, and the issue of balance will probably never be settled definitively. Each period brings its own cases of conflict between the rights of the collective and those of the individual—the right for the community to know about the lives of public figures versus the right to privacy being just one of many examples.

Here again, the specifics will emerge only after informed and lively debate on each issue. We must, however, keep in mind that few rights are absolute—their limits end when they begin to encroach upon another set of rights. As one classic example has it, "Freedom of speech does not give a person permission to shout 'Fire!' in a crowded theater." (Unless of course there really is a fire.) Obviously the laws and courts of our system of justice have focused on this issue from the beginning. It would be much easier to manage this abstraction, however, if we more thoroughly educated all citizens in the principles and problems of the matter.

Here is another key principle:

HUMANS ARE NOT THE SOLE LIFE FORM ON OUR LIVING EARTH. ALL OTHER LIVING CREATURES ARE PART OF A SYNERGISTIC WHOLE, AND THEY ARE PARTS OF THE CONSCIOUSNESS OF OUR PLANET. MAN, AS THE HIGHEST CONSCIOUSNESS OF THE EARTH, MUST SUPPORT THE TOTAL LIFE PROCESS OF THE PLANET.

Just consider for a moment the probable outcome of a context that held sacred the above principle as opposed to contexts in which mindsets allow for the destruction of the ionosphere, the cutting off of our oxygen supply through excessive cutting of forests, the wasting of natural resources, the killing off of entire species of earth's creatures, and irresponsible overpopulation.

The natural environment of the planet is the climate in which we all conduct our lives. We may assume that every species and every natural condition has some purpose, and that we must find our place within a context that is health-producing for all that nature has afforded us. To do otherwise will be to jeopardize our own survival, for one day or another all the devastation that we have wrought to the planet's natural systems will combine to choke off our own existence as a species.

A FUTURE CODE OF ETHICS

In a psychologically healthy society, leaders would consider themselves servants of society. Whether they so consider themselves or not, however, it is now indisputable that leadership is the *sine qua non* integrating and directing force in our midst, without which our complex society can no longer continue to function effectively. Therefore, people have no option but to delegate authority to leaders and to submit themselves to that authority.

However, we are on a two-way street; leaders are obliged to hold followers' lives and futures in sacred trust. "Their" leadership has actually been created by the needs of the people and exists as a service to the people.

What would happen if all leaders saw themselves as servants rather than as rulers, controllers, and manipulators? What would happen if they saw their reason for being as leading people to outcomes that kept society healthy and working for the common good of all, rather than for the narrow good of a few? Among other things this context would require a radical letting go of the myopic view that leaders are entitled to operate primarily to achieve prominence, power, or material rewards. It would mean forgoing the view that because they are "in charge" they may arrogate to themselves the "right" to run their operations to suit their own needs rather than to fit implicit social needs, which leader roles are created to serve.

The ultimate expression of leaders running things to suit their own needs was slavery. In the early industrial revolution this mindset resulted in rank exploitation of labor that put many workers in slave-like conditions and necessitated the creation of child labor laws. More recently business leaders who thought their roles gave them a rightful power to feather their own nests have engaged in price fixing, monopoly, restraint of trade, sabotage of unions, and manipulating government. In the public sector, societies have had to endure heads of government who channeled wealth into their private holdings, not unlike executives in business who pay themselves exorbitant bonuses, even when their companies may not be doing well. Such behavior reflects inappropriate mindsets; different behavior can be expected to follow from new mindsets.

When a World Professional Leadership Association becomes active, one of its missions will be to adopt an ethical code that reflects healthy new mindsets. Following are suggested tenets for leaders to consider inscribing in such a code:

> SINCE LEADERSHIP IS A ROLE OF SERVICE AND OF RESPONSIBILITY TOWARD THE COMMON GOOD, IT SHALL BE UNETHICAL FOR PERSONS TO PRACTICE LEADERSHIP FOR WHICH THEY HAVE NOT ACQUIRED THE NECESSARY TRAINING AND SKILLS AND OTHERWISE MET THE CRITERIA ESTABLISHED BY THEIR PEERS AS PROFESSIONAL STANDARDS.

We have already reviewed in depth the idea of leaders as servants of the wider society. Here I am only adding that this notion of servant is not something optional, or just "a good idea;" it must be at the heart of any approach to reforming leadership.

Leadership has an inevitable and profound impact upon other leaders, followers, and society in general. For the most part, however, followers lack the knowledge and data to judge the quality and appropriateness of the leadership they are receiving. Often, they can judge that quality only by experiencing its after-the-fact consequences. They must, therefore, be protected from abuses of leadership by the ethical commitment of those who step forward to lead.

As is true with the medical and legal professions, people must place themselves in the hands of leaders in order to get what they need in life. And they must do so without much ability to evaluate professional qualifications. That is why leaders, like doctors and lawyers, must not practice without the requisite training and skills.

> IT SHALL BE UNETHICAL FOR A LEADER TO IMPINGE UPON THE RIGHTS OF FOLLOWERS BY EXTENDING POWER GRANTED FOR USE IN THE LEADERSHIP ROLE TO THINGS BEYOND THOSE INHERENT IN THE PURPOSEFUL OPERATION OF THAT ROLE.

In no way should leaders demonstrate by any policy or behavior that they are socially or personally more powerful than the people they lead. One common example of workplace abuse, which has begun to receive well-deserved attention, is sexual harassment, which includes any subtle demand for sexual compliance. In all but a few cases this form of abuse has been applied against female staff by male bosses. However, other nonsexual, but nevertheless abusive, practices by superiors who require that their subordinates "please" them personally can no longer be tolerated. Followers have a right to advancement if they perform their jobs well and generally mesh well with their coworkers; they should not be held to some extra standard of "pleasing" the boss. Much more must be done to assure that bosses and workers are considered equal in dignity and in their human rights.

By virtue of their privileged positions, leaders are frequently able to take advantage of opportunities for personal gain beyond the assigned pay and perquisites of their positions. Neither followers nor the leadership matrix are well served by such inappropriate decisions and actions. In recent years the entire savings and loan industry was damaged by people who sought personal advantage from their positions. An ethical code promulgated by a professional association would go far toward eliminating such offenses against society.

A LEADER SHALL BE ETHICALLY REQUIRED TO SERVE HIS OR HER MATRIX IN A MANNER THAT IS ALSO LEAST DAMAGING TO, AND MOST SUPPORTIVE OF, ESSENTIAL ASPECTS OF SOCIETY. BECAUSE THERE IS A COMPLEX RELATIONSHIP BETWEEN THE PARTS AND THE WHOLE OF SOCIETY, IT IS OFTEN DIFFICULT TO DETERMINE WHICH OF ALTERNATIVE PATHS IS, IN FACT, THE BEST PATH. IN ANY EVENT, HOWEVER, IT SHALL BE UNETHICAL NOT TO TAKE ALL POSSIBLE STEPS TO FOLLOW THE PATH OF LEAST HARM.

We already know and agree that it is unethical to bolster a company's profits by dumping toxic wastes into public waters. However, there remain vast areas to explore where ethical standards are not yet clear. One area includes all industrial processes that pollute air or water or destroy the ozone layer that protects the earth from the searing infra-red rays of the sun. Another area involves executive compensation. What about executives who pay themselves huge salaries and bonuses even though profits are down and they are laying off workers? On another theme, is it ethical for the U.S. Department of Agriculture to provide subsidies for exporting American tobacco overseas while other branches of the same federal government mount domestic campaigns to reduce smoking? And, is it unethical for Congress not to provide subsidies to help tobacco farmers and producers make a switch to another means of earning a living? The issues in such ethical quandaries must be worked out on a case-by-case basis and choices made through democratic processes.

LEADERS MAY NOT MIS-REPRESENT THEIR INTENTIONS, THEIR COMPANIES, OR A CURRENT OR FUTURE STATE OF AFFAIRS IN ORDER TO INDUCE PEOPLE TO BECOME THEIR FOLLOWERS.

Many people in our society join companies or organizations, or in other ways become followers, because they perceive this or that matrix as an avenue to pursue goals they value, such as stability, good earning power, or a healthy work atmosphere. Often, they do so because a leader presents "facts" about that company or organization. Since the applicant frequently has no adequate means of evaluating a company other than the leader's word, the applicant is dependent upon a fair representation of reality by a recruiting leader. Under the high ethical standards that we will need for supra-leadership, leaders would be enjoined from exaggerations or gross misrepresentations of the conditions or prospects for the company.

IT SHALL BE UNETHICAL FOR A LEADER NOT TO BE TRUTHFUL ABOUT HIS OR HER EVALUATION OF A FOLLOWER'S PERFORMANCE IN ANY ORGANIZATIONAL SETTING WHERE QUALITY OF PERFORMANCE, OR A LEADER'S JUDGMENT ABOUT IT, HAS SIGNIFCANT EFFECTS UPON THE FOLLOWER'S CAREER OR UPON THE FOLLOWER'S PRESENT OR FUTURE LIFE.

All too often I hear the complaint, "If I had known they were so upset about this or that, I could have made some changes and kept my job!" Inaccurate or incomplete presentations to an employee of the true state of management's evaluation of that person's efforts has not yet been made a sufficiently important issue. Lives are sidetracked and whole families often suffer needlessly just because management is less than forthcoming about job performances until just before people are laid off or fired for subpar work quality. Such conduct by management is abusive and can no longer be considered ethical.

IT IS UNDERSTOOD THAT A LEADER'S PRIMARY RESPONSIBILITY SHALL BE TO SUSTAIN OR INCREASE THE EFFECTIVENESS AND SUCCESS OF HIS OR HER AREA OF RESPONSIBILITY. NONETHELESS, IT SHALL BE UNETHICAL FOR A LEADER TO AIM FOR THAT RESULT WITHOUT A REASONABLE ATTEMPT TO BALANCE OUT THAT GOAL WITH SUPPORT FOR THE GROWTH, CAREER DEVELOPMENT, AND PERSONAL LIFE OUTCOMES OF ALL FOLLOWERS OF THAT LEADER.

Most of us do not work independently to get what we need. Instead, we participate as members of large, working collectives in a complex social system. The steppingstones to many of our life goals are through organizational systems controlled by leaders. Therefore, every leader is responsible not only for making his or her leadership matrix productive, but also for helping all subordinates expand their skills and earning capabilities so they can pursue personal growth and job satisfaction.

SINCE ALL LEADERSHIP HAS A SHAPING IMPACT ON FOLLOWER MINDSETS, IT SHALL BE UNETHICAL FOR LEADERS TO LEAD IN A MANNER THAT GENERATES MINDSETS NEGATIVE TO THE WELL-BEING OF SOCIETY OR TO THE WELL-BEING OF THE FOLLOWERS. THE ETHICAL LEADER IS EXPECTED TO FOSTER SOCIALLY SUPPORTIVE MINDSETS, SELF RESPECT IN FOLLOWERS, AND TRUST IN THE PROFESSION OF LEADERSHIP.

Dignity is key. In no way should followers be commanded or induced to perform work that lowers their dignity as human beings. Nor should they be required to perform otherwise dignified work in such a way that they feel exploited.

The final point in this proposed text of an ethical code for leaders points to the effects leaders themselves have on the viability of their profession. For the most part leaders have not until now given much thought as to how they may be influencing followers' conceptions of leaders or leadership. However, if followers in a given matrix constantly complain of "tyrants" or "monsters," the fault falls squarely on superiors who are not bringing honor to the profession of leadership. Therefore, anyone who aspires to a role as leader and anyone who currently lives with such a role will do himself or herself, and society at large, a tremendous service by subscribing to a code of ethics for the profession of leadership.

BIBLIOGRAPHY

Assagioli, Roberto, *Psychokinesis: A Manual of Principles and Techniques*: NY: Viking, 1971.

Bennis, Warren, *Why Leaders Can't Lead*, SF: Jossey-Bass, 1989.

Berry, Thomas, *The Dream of the Earth*, SF: Sierra Club Books, 1988.

DePree, Max, *The Jazz of Leadership*, NY: Doubleday, 1992.

Galbraith, John Kenneth, *The Age of Uncertainty*, Boston: Houghton-Mifflin, 1977.

Gardner, John, *On Leadership*, NY: The Free Press, 1990.

—*Self Renewal: The Individual and the Innovative Society*, NY: Norton, 1981.

Goleman, Daniel, *Emotional Intelligence*, NY: Bantam Books, 1995.

Handy, Charles, The Age of Unreason, Boston: Harvard Business School Press, 1989.

— *The Age of Paradox*, Boston, Harvard Business School Press, 1995.

Kennedy, Paul, *Preparing for the Twenty-First Century*, NY: Random House, 1993.

Meadows, Dennis and Donella et al, *Limits to Growth*, NY: Universe Books, 1972.

Peters, Thomas J., *Thriving on Chaos*, NY: Knopf, 1987.

Postman, Neil, *Technopoly: The Surrender of Culture to Technology*, NY: Knopf, 1992.

Senge, Peter, *The Fifth Discipline: The Art and Practice of the Learning Organization*, NY: Doubleday-Currency, 1990.

Wheatley, Margaret, *Leadership and the New Science*, SF: Berrett-Koehler, 1992.

INDEX

A

AA model, 53
aborigines, Australian, 71
abortion rights, 100
Abraham Lincoln, President, 178
accountability, 14
accreditation for leaders, 166
achiever, 147
acid rain, 14, 83, 110
acquisitiveness, 142
Action Commands, 85, 79, 85
Adams, Abigail, 109
advertising, 88, 181
aerosol sprays, 64
Airline controllers, 67
Al Capp, 121
alcohol, 53, 75
Alexander the Great, 103
aliveness, 7, 27, 37, 44, 46, 133
American culture, 52
American Revolution, 72
American social fabric, 144
anarchists, 99
Apartheid, 151
armed forces, 56
Assagioli, Roberto, 37, 54
authoritarian leadership, 154
authority, 2, 16, 17, 52, 59,
    113, 129, 154, 168, 184
authority structures, 154
automated mind operations,
    28, 135
automated minds, 25, 38
automated programs, 23, 24, 126
automated tapes, 22
automated thinking, 8
automatic mindsets, 33, 38
automatic pilot, 8, 90, 107
automatic responses, 97, 138

automatic social reflexes, 153
automation, 23, 126, 170
Awareness, 29
awareness, 11, 13, 23, 25, 27,
    29, 30, 32, 33, 37, 44, 46,
    49, 52, 53, 55, 65, 80, 88,
    89, 92, 94, 97, 102, 116, 126,
    127, 129, 132, 133, 135, 136,
    137, 138, 139, 140, 141, 144,
    146, 152, 153, 154, 166, 167,
    168, 181, 182

B

bacterial warfare, 112
banking, world, 67
Basic biological programs, 19
BBC, 82
being-awareness, 50
Being-consciousness, 37, 132, 133,
    136, 137, 139, 140, 142
belief system, 47
Berlin Wall, 8, 151
bid rigging, 106
body politic, 144
bootstrapping, 160
bootstraps, 160
boredom, 143, 170
boundaries, 34, 37, 86
Boy Scouts, 122
Branch Davidians, 53
breakdowns (in institutions), 10
Burke, Edmund, 106
Bush, President George, 65, 66
business administration, degree
    of, 159

C

California, 175
cancer study, 93

INDEX

INDEX

ABOUT THE AUTHOR

James N. Farr holds the Ph.D. in counseling psychology from the University of Minnesota. He taught and directed graduate studies at New York University, was the first director of the Center for Creative Leadership in Greensboro, North Carolina, and for forty years headed Farr Associates, Inc., a firm specializing in leadership development. He has published articles in *Executive Excellence, Business Leader* and other journals. He is currently at work on three other books.

Dr. Farr welcomes your letters and comments. Please write him at:

> 7622 Royster Rd.
> Greensboro, NC 27455

Or reach him via e-mail: drfarr@leadership-trust.org